Over The Hills And Away

The Life and Times of Thomas Norris

1778 – 1858

Daren Wayne Norris

To Trevor with very best wishes

WRITERSWORLD

United Kingdom • France • Germany • Spain

Over The Hills and Far Away

By

Daren Wayne Norris

Copyright © 2005

ISBN 1-904181-74-0

Copyedited by Richard Sexton

WRITERSWORLD
9 Manor Court
Enstone
Oxfordshire,
OX7 4LU
England
www.writersworld.co.uk

Daren Wayne Norris

- Prologue -

After some sixteen years of research the author presents this account of the life and times of his Great, Great, Great Grandfather Thomas Norris who was born in Watford in 1778 and who served with the 57th of Foot, (The West Middlesex Regiment) from 1803 to 1816. This book charts all the major events of Thomas's very colourful and courageous life and in particular it retraces his steps in the Peninsula War against Napoleon's "Grande Armie" in the early part of the nineteenth century. Private Thomas Norris was present at the famous and seemingly impossible British victory at the battle of Albuhera in western Spain. Outnumbered almost five to one, this is where the 57th regiment earned their nickname "the Die Hards" due to their distinction in battle and heavy losses on the 16th May 1811. By the end of this terrible engagement, two thirds of the regiment lay strewn across the battlefield, all with their wounds to the front. The battle honour 'ALBUHERA' was to remain synonymous with this proud regiment for over 160 years until its eventual disbandment in 1973. The Princess of Wales's Royal Regiment maintains the anniversary of this battle as a prominent date in the military calendar, with a full service of remembrance at St Paul's Cathedral on "Albuhera Day" each year. Thomas Norris went on to fight with the 57ᵗʰ Regiment at the other famous Peninsula battles of Vittoria, The Pyrenees, Nive, Nivelle and Toulouse, emerging victorious in each of them and finally forcing Napoleon's abdication in 1814.

During the course of this research, the author and his brother visited the village at Albuhera or "La Albuera" as it is known in Spain. They have developed a strong and lasting relationship with the locals, who now regard them as part of what they call "El Famillia Grande" – The Big Family. The battle is powerfully re-enacted in Napoleonic period costume by local families and visitors from abroad on the anniversary, attracting thousands of people to this remote and very beautiful region of Spain each year. The British continue to be held in high esteem due to the efforts of our ancestors in helping to free Spain from French rule all those years ago. This is one place in the world we can still be proud to say we are British. This book goes on to explain the various genealogical research techniques used to trace accurately the story of Thomas's life and gives a brief history of the regiment with which he served.

A donation will be made from the proceeds of this book to help fund urgent renovation and maintenance work at the British Army cemetery at the Chapel of San Juan in Elvas, Portugal, where those lost in the battle of Albuhera were taken for burial almost 200 years ago. These are thought to be among the oldest British Army war graves in existence. A service is held at the chapel in May each year to coincide with the annual week of Napoleonic themed festivities at La Albuera, just a few miles away. A contribution will also be made from the proceeds to help fund the battle museum at the main village square in La Albuera. Please accept my sincere thanks for supporting this cause, which has been arranged in association with Celia Denney, Secretary of the "Friends of the British Cemetery at Elvas" charity, residing in the region. By a shear streak of coincidence, Celia Denney was also born in Watford.

Particular thanks also go to The National Archive, The National Army Museum, The Royal Hospital Chelsea, The Princess of Wales's Royal Regiment, The Middlesex Regimental Association, The Public Records Office, Kew and of course the many villagers of La Albuera who have helped this story to come alive.

*"Retracing local heroes of the past…
This remarkable history of the battle
at Albuhera has been meticulously
traced by an ancestor of one of the
British soldiers fighting in the battle,
Thomas Norris."*

**Matt Hemley,
Watford Observer Newspaper
(July 2004).**

"The Die-Hards at Albuhera"

Many thanks to Jamie Thornton, a gifted military artist in the UK specialising in the Napoleonic period, for kindly allowing his painting "The Die-Hards at Albuhera" to be used for the cover of this book. This is a wonderful piece of work which I believe really captures the spirit and conditions of the time. Mr Thornton has also kindly provided copies of this artwork which were presented to the British Napoleonic re-enactment regiment in Spain, where a print is now proudly mounted in the 57th mess at the Albuera battlefield site. Limited edition prints can be obtained direct from the artist via his internet website at

http://www.webspawner.com/users/napoleonicart/index.html

CONTENTS

Dedication

1. Dedication

Before we embark upon this literary voyage through the years which shaped Britain and the wider modern world, spare a thought for a man who made much of the journey possible. Brian Norris, my Uncle, spent most of the early 1990's researching our ancestors, thumbing through endless parish registers, wills and military documents, trying to piece together the recorded life of Thomas Norris. He exhausted every available source of information in the pursuit of a true account proving lineage, and credit therefore goes to him for carrying out and funding much of the necessary detailed, laborious genealogical research work. True to his usual meticulous form, he produced clear and concise records which are fully catalogued and cross-referenced at every possible opportunity to leave no doubt in one's mind as to the relevance, accuracy and authenticity of the historical documents cited.

Brian, affectionately known as 'UB' to his nephews, was born in Watford in April 1933, the third child of Sydney and Lily Norris, my paternal Grandparents. He was nine years older than my father and by the early 1940s, he was charged with the responsibility of raising his new brother, whilst his father commanded the Hertfordshire branch of the Auxiliary Fire Service as Chief Fire Officer during the blitz in London. Brian's mother Lily had suffered with psychological problems for many years, and was in no fit state to provide proper care for her children, the eldest of whom was Reginald (nicknamed Ginger) aged about thirteen at the time. I remember Uncle Brian recalling one warm September evening in 1940, when, whilst sitting on the roof of a pre-cast concrete shed in the back garden of the family residence in Gorle Close, he gazed with disbelief across the horizon. A burning red and amber glow radiated in the south eastern sky. The blitz had begun and his father Sydney was in the centre of it.

After the Second World War, Brian grew up in North Watford with the family remaining at Gorle Close. He excelled at school earning his early nick name "Prof" following several explosions and hilarious events centring on his chemistry experiments in the kitchen. I understand from various accounts that on one occasion, this resulted in the back door being blown off its hinges!

Brian joined the army in his late teens, working on intelligence operations in Egypt from about 1950. His brother Ginger, himself a bombardier, was captured and taken prisoner by the Chinese in Korea, so Brian requested a posting there in order to help find his brother. Ginger managed to escape his captors just as Brian arrived with part of the Gloucestershire Regiment, ill-attired for the harsh Korean winter in his light Egyptian desert kit. While serving in Korea, Brian was involved in a British action where his small battalion held off a huge force of several thousand Chinese troops until they were finally overrun and the order "every man for himself" was given. During the mass retreat, Brian apparently spent several days hiding in a cave along with a handful of others who had followed him. While there he discovered a skeleton wearing a Gloucestershire Regiment uniform, with the tell–tail "fore and aft" cap badges. One can only assume it was one of the poor souls who never made it out following the previous, more famous Gloucestershire Regiment retreat some months earlier - known to history as the action at "Gloucester Valley". Not surprisingly, Brian didn't talk much about his service in Korea and I'm sure he would much rather have been able to forget some of the horrors he must have witnessed.

He married Isobel in Watford and in time, emigrated to Rhodesia (now Zimbabwe) with his young family. Brian's sheet metal working business was a success and the family enjoyed many happy years overseas. I met Brian for the first time during his visit to England in the summer of 1974, when I was just six years old. Uncle Brian had come to England for a few weeks, and my mother had brought him to meet my brother Brian and me from school. Mum arrived at the school entrance with a man that looked not unlike my Grandfather from the back, as he had turned away in an attempt to surprise us when we came out. Mum asked us to guess who this curious man was.

"Granddad" we both shouted and cheered, such was our affection for him. "No" Mum said, "it's your Uncle Brian from Rhodesia". The stories about Uncle Brian living in Africa came flooding back in our minds. This man was to us Tarzan Lord of the Jungle. We all joined hands and walked to the sweet shop on Tolpits Lane. Uncle Brian bought so much confectionary that the shop assistant had to pile it all into a black plastic sack about the size of a dustbin liner. My uncle produced a crisp five pound note and paid without flinching. Not something I'd seen done before! I knew from that time onwards, my Uncle and I were going to be firm friends. Everyone was in awe of him during his stay. Family, friends and even people passing him in the street were intrigued and impressed by what they saw and listened to – well, I suppose he did stand out in a crowd wearing his safari suit and bushman's hat, telling stories about the Tiger Fish that drowned a man back home! I remember after a week or two, when Uncle Brian was leaving to return to Rhodesia my nine year old next door neighbour Paul Scott helped him with his bags to the bus stop on Croxley View. Paul was rewarded with a shining 50p coin which I can still picture catching the sunlight on that bright morning. My pocket money at the time was about 5p a week if I was lucky, so you can imagine the beaming smile on my neighbour's face. Brian, Isobel and their youngest children moved back to England in about 1980, due to the troubles in Rhodesia in the run-up to independence from Britain. This is when I really got to know Brian and his family. I spent two weeks working with Uncle Brian during the summer months of 1984, at his catering business in Bedfordshire. We had a great time despite the hard work. I grew to know and love his family, and our special relationship has always been very dear to me. Not so much an Uncle as a friend.

Uncle Brian carving a spit-roasted ox at his daughter Meryl's wedding in Rhodesia.

This book is therefore dedicated to my Uncle Brian for both his friendship and his inspiration, without which this paper would have remained un-blotted.

Sadly, Uncle Brian passed away in the early hours of 24th May 1996, before this book could be completed. Memories of Uncle Brian will always be immeasurably dear to me and I am forever grateful to have had the love, friendship and inspiration of this exceptional man who signed himself simply "B".

God bless him.

Daren Norris
Sept 2001.

Introduction

2. Introduction

It is likely you have picked up this book due to an interest in the histories of either the Norris family or the Middlesex Regiment, or perhaps you have an interest in genealogy generally and want to find out how to begin researching your family tree. Many readers may purely have an interest in the battle of Albuhera and the British involvement in the Peninsula War. In writing, I have tried to satisfy all these groups by highlighting particular points of interest along with details of any material sources and of course their specific relevance to the story of Thomas's life. It is important to note that while I have included much information gleaned from army records and numerous other military sources, this book is not intended to be an authoritative work on military history or warfare as I am by no means an expert on these subjects. On the other hand, for those related to the Norris line and those associated with the Middlesex Regiment, this may become a treasured possession to be preserved for future generations so that they may learn the proud history of our country, our regiment, and our name. This book sets out a very brief history of the Norris family so far, before telling the story of Thomas's life and exploring the history of the regiment he served with during the Napoleonic period.

Probably, like me, many is the time you will have opened a book, read a few lines or pages, then lost interest and given it up. The problem is that it takes such an enormous effort for human beings to commit themselves to a task, challenge or even a relationship, unless there is some kind of reward on offer. This is human nature after all. I must admit this has not always been the most exciting subject in the world to write about, so please do bear with me as I have tried to make this book as readable as possible without wallowing in too much detail. The reward for your efforts will be the opportunity for you to really understand the subject and truly know from whence you came. This book will also provide the reader with a wealth of general reference information on a wide range of subjects, particularly those pertaining to the history of our great nation.

My original interest in the history of our family was born out of a dream I had when I was about seven years old. I dreamt that for some reason I had died in adulthood and as part of my initiation to the afterlife, I was guided by a spirit to a large, dark room where all my ancestors stood shoulder to shoulder in a long line. The spirit introduced me to each of my ancestors individually and I shook hands with them. As I walked along the line, some of them were dressed in fine mediaeval clothes, some in armour, some were covered in cobwebs. Some appeared to be craftsmen and others were wounded soldiers. The last person I was introduced to was my Grandfather Sydney Norris, who had died a year or two before. He seemed to recognise me, and it was my turn to join the end of the line. Strangely though, I stood next to my Grandfather, not my Father as one might have expected. This dream stayed with me for many years, probably because of the loss of my Grandfather, but also because I was concerned that in my dream I seemed to have died before my Father at quite an early age.

After that, I became more and more curious about my ancestors and wanted to know the history of our family so that in time, I could eventually pass the knowledge down to my own children when I grew up. In about February 1989, at the age of 20, I decided to start tracing our family history. I didn't know of any elderly Norris relatives still living and so had to rely on the limited information available, which was basically my Grandfather's name and year of birth. I visited the then Public Records Office at St Catherine's House in Holborn and found a birth registration for Sydney Herbert Norris in 1903. I ordered a copy of the certificate, and when it arrived at home by post, I found this Sydney's father was Henry Norris. I told my parents and Uncle Brian all about it, and how I was going to pursue this as a hobby as far back in time as possible. Uncle Brian was very enthusiastic and got involved straight away by talking to his cousin Triss Davies (my Great Aunt

Bertha's daughter) who had some old photographs and birth certificates. Triss told Uncle Brian that my Grandfather's Father (my Great Grandfather) was not Henry Norris. She believed his name was George. The certificate I had obtained from the PRO Holborn was the wrong one, and upon checking there again, there were indeed two Sydney Herbert Norris's born in 1903. One in Walthamstow, West Ham whose father was Henry Norris, and the other was in Watford – my Grandfather Sydney, whose father was George Norris. This set the ball rolling properly, and Uncle Brian and I became quite addicted to the pursuit of further information from which to draw up a family tree going as far back in time as possible. As mentioned in my earlier dedication to him, my Uncle Brian carried out an extraordinary amount of detailed research in the early to mid 1990's but sadly passed away in 1996, leaving me to continue our research alone when the availability of time permitted. The usual priorities of family, studies and career have demanded much of my time since then and it is only now some nine years later, and sixteen years since beginning this quest that I am at last able to proudly publish this book. This is the story of the life and times of my Great, Great, Great Grandfather Thomas Norris who was born in my home town of Watford in September 1778 and who served with the 57th of Foot in their finest hour at the Battle of Albuhera.

Thomas came from a long line of Norris's in Hertfordshire and was one of the second of eight consecutive generations of our family to have lived in Watford. This long-lasting connection with Hertfordshire (at least thirteen consecutive generations in all) has made my local research all the more interesting from a personal point of view and has enabled me to more closely study the lives and haunts of my ancestors. It is particularly satisfying to be able to show my children some of the places their ancestors lived and worked in the distant past and for them to touch their history at first hand. I hope in time that this information will be passed to further generations of our family and so leave something of a legacy to be remembered, added to and maintained for years to come. As the research into Thomas's life progressed over many years, we found more and more information available in military records held at the Public Records Office in Kew. These give enormous personal detail about Thomas and his whereabouts throughout much of his army service and time as a Chelsea Pensioner. With so much good information available, breathing life into Thomas's story, I felt compelled to compile a book of my findings to more easily share and narrate this extraordinary man's biography.

I put together a large ring binder of information over many years and from time to time I'd take it out to show various members of the family and interested friends. Every now and then I would do some more research and little by little add to the folder. This went on for several years and by 2002, although I had always intended to write a book about Thomas, I had almost given up my research due to other commitments. In February 2004, my brother Paul visited me at home with his family and the subject of Thomas came in to the conversation. I took out the ring binder to show Paul some of the copies of old military documents and noted that the famous battle of Albuhera was fought on 16th May. I suggested that we visit La Albuera on the anniversary of the battle to pay our respects and to get an idea of what the place looked like. Paul agreed and we immediately set about making plans to travel to Spain in May. We initially considered arranging visits to the major Peninsula battlefields of Talavera, Salamanca and Vittoria, as well as the fortress cities of Badajoz and Cuidad Rodrigo. We also wanted to spend some time in Barcelona and Madrid, but with just four days to pack this in, it proved too adventurous a plan given the amount of travelling involved. Having purchased maps, guides and a couple of Spanish phrase books, we settled on a more realistic itinerary with advice from our friends Linda and Trevor Hacking who have previously lived in Spain themselves.

On 14th May we flew from London Gatwick to Madrid and spent a memorable evening at the Plaza del Sol in the company of the singer Bonnie Tyler, who was giving a public performance in the open square. The next day, we took a taxi to Madrid's Puerto de Atocha station, the scene of terrorist bombings some weeks earlier and observed a few minutes silence as a mark of respect for the victims and their families. We then travelled for about eight hours cross-country by train to the mediaeval fortress city of Badajoz in

Extremadura. From there we took a local bus for the remaining 12 mile south easterly drive to the remote village of La Albuera. As you will see, this was the beginning of a very different kind of journey. I hope you enjoy the ride.

A Letter from Spain

3. A Letter from Spain

During our brief stay in La Albuera we made friends with many of the local Spanish inhabitants and visiting members of the Middlesex Regiment. Our time there was full of wonderful experiences and coincidences, which I recorded in a letter to Colonel Peter Knox during our return train journey from Badajoz to Madrid and I have included the major part of its contents here to help set the scene…

"Dear Colonel Peter,

I am writing this letter from my seat on the 0735hrs train from Badajoz to Madrid on Monday 17th May 2004, so please do excuse my composition and try to bear with me here. We are just pulling out of Caceres railway station, having read the local newspaper "Hoy" Diario De Extremadura – well, perhaps 'read' is not the word to use as 'Mi no habla mucho Espanol' as you well know Sir. Anyway, thanks to your kind invitation to lunch at Albuera and provision of transport to Badajoz, we are well on our way home. My brother and I send sincere thanks for your most generous hospitality and good company.

As I mentioned in my brief anecdotes on the coach, my brother Paul and I made our way independently to Albuera in order to pay our respects at the battlefield as we knew from my earlier research and that undertaken by my late Uncle Brian, that the anniversary of the battle was on the 16ᵗʰ May. We were however completely unaware that the village or the regiment celebrated the anniversary of the battle – either in Spain or in the UK. We had expected to find a remote rural village with a handful of villas and perhaps a monument to the 57ᵗʰ as their distinction on the battlefield has been so well documented. We arrived in Albuera by bus from Badajoz on Saturday afternoon, having left Watford at 0400hrs Friday, only to find that the hotel had lost our reservation details and did not have room for us. The hotel had no reception and we had to contact the proprietor via Linda Hacking, a Spanish-speaking friend in the UK. At this point, we were expecting to have to sleep in a field under the stars, but thankfully with Linda's help the language barrier was breached and we managed to get basic accommodation for the night, albeit at quite a premium.

During the course of the evening the village started to awaken. A small stream of Spaniards began to trickle down the main road, the "Avenida de Extremedura" in the general direction of the battlefield. More and more people filled the pavements and the gentle stream of locals was joined by many others dressed in nineteenth century style military uniforms. It seems that on the anniversary each year, the various families in the village are expected to represent a number of foreign and Spanish regiments which fought at the battle, including the 57ᵗʰ. We followed these very welcoming and friendly people along the Avenida, across a river-bridge to a bull ring opposite the battlefield which doubles as an amphitheatre. *A very professional theatre company staged "La Albuera: Historia de amor y muerte", which is apparently a very popular Spanish love story about a British soldier and a local girl during the time of the battle. It was a spectacular performance and very similar to RSC. Of course it was all in Spanish, but we followed the 'Romeo and Juliet' tragic love story theme, which ended with 'John Smith' the British soldier being killed at the battle of Albuera. Very sad and not a dry eye in the house. We were the only British there on the night and were invited to join the Spaniards in British redcoat uniforms for a drink at their regimental mess behind the bullring area. Of course we agreed and made friends immediately upon finding that their mess was built in honour of the 57th and is adorned with all kinds of memorabilia and the Middlesex Regimental insignia.*

As with yourself, I explained our genealogical link with the 57th and specifically that our Great, Great, Great Grandfather Thomas Norris fought with the regiment alongside the Spanish at the battle of Albuera some 193 years before. The Spanish 'representative' Captain of those dressed as British Redcoats – a Senor Miguel Gomez along with his family and friends welcomed us in and very kindly prepared a light meal of feta cheese, olives, Iberian ham, and fresh bread, charging our glasses with endless supplies of their delightful local vino tinto and ice cold cerveza. This was delicious and the festivities began in earnest with typical Spanish music, singing, dancing and a wondrous atmosphere of anticipation.

At midnight, I was marched out of the mess in to the fiesta court, a large rectangular area of hard standing about the size of a football field surrounded by numerous other representative foreign regimental messes – which were teaming with yet more people in period costume. Senor Gomez took out an antique flintlock pistol, loaded it with gunpowder, tamped down the wading and added a cap to the firing mechanism. He took my hand and forced the pistol into it holding my arm high and straight. I was asked to fire the gun. As I said before, my Spanish is not very good, but I instinctively knew what to say and do. There was obviously something very significant about it being midnight and me standing in a line of Spaniards dressed in British uniforms, all holding what appeared to be replica Brown Bess muskets. A little of Shakespeare's Henry V at Agincourt came to me and with full lungs I shouted:

"GOD SAVE THE QUEEN, ENGLAND AND SAINT GEORGE" *then*
"VIVA ESPAÑA, VIVA GRAN BRETAÑA"

As I fired the gun they all repeated my words at the top of their voices in a salute to the 57th. The sound of the gun resonated through the fiesta court and out to the open fields – everything stopped in silence, just for a few moments.

Each of the regiments, that is to say the local Spaniards and hundreds of foreigners dressed as British, French, Portuguese, German, Polish and of course Spanish, began to fall-in. Each regiment representation consisted of about six to ten men and an officer. All the regiments paraded around the fiesta court and the square in front of the bullring with full drums playing. The Union Jack was held highest of all the flags by Senor Miguel Gomez and the regiment were ordered eyes right and saluted my brother and I as they marched past. Paul and I obviously stood tall and saluted back, a single tear held in each eye and our hearts bursting with pride. After much emotion the various regiments fell-out, the representative 57th threw their arms around us and we continued with the former celebrations and festivities in the 57th mess until 0330hrs Sunday morning. Paul and I then retired to our accommodation, but the Spaniards went on until around 0800hrs!

On Sunday morning we arose a little later than we had hoped and made our way to the nearest café for a somewhat tardy but much needed breakfast of fried pigeon with lemon and salt served with more goats cheese and Iberian ham – typical elevenses in Albuera apparently, and really quite good. This is when we met the earliest arrivals of the Middlesex contingent, happily including as you may recall, your good self.

Fortune shone on us once again and after following your kind directions to the battlefield and ridge, we later returned to the village centre for the solemn, moving service to bury the old Middlesex colours brought from St Paul's Cathedral in London. Our Spanish friends again joined us for a brief time after the service before

Paul and I boarded the coach to travel with your selves to lunch opposite the ridge. We had the great privilege of being formally introduced to many distinguished guests including; the Mayor of La Albuera - Don Manuel Diaz González , Brigadier Richard Holmes, Her Majesty the Queen's Military Attaché to Spain and of course the many, many loyal members of the Middlesex Regiment and their families, with whom we swapped contact details in the hope of fostering a continued relationship.

It seems an impossible coincidence that all this could happen to us – but clearly this was meant to be. The local Spanish population and those in the wider Extremadura area have an affinity, perhaps even feel a kinship with the British and they truly appreciate what our forefathers did to help secure their freedom from French rule. These people live and breathe what happened in the past, and this is something our own community could learn and benefit from. History lessons at school for me only ever focused on Spain as the aggressor and the eternal enemy for making an attempt on our own freedom during the days of the Spanish Armada and Trafalgar. On coming to Spain we find they are our brothers in arms in more ways than one. There is much to be done and much we can do to enhance and re-establish the honourable, respectable qualities with which the British were formerly associated in Europe. To this end, my brother Paul and I hereby pledge our allegiance to the Middlesex Regiment and undertake to support and attend future celebrations each year – God willing. Our children will inherit this history, and they along with their descendants will maintain the immortal memory of 'the Die-Hards' continuing to make the silent toast on Albuhera Day each year – even when we are dust. There are no words in English or in Spanish for that matter to convey just how powerful and unexpected this monumental experience has been.

Please accept our heartfelt thanks for your kind hospitality and for being part of this wonderful story. I apologise for the length of this correspondence, however I do feel it is important to formally record and preserve the memory of these very special events for future generations – this may help them carry a brighter torch for Great Britain throughout our future in Europe. We are now already part of this rich and proud history, and although of short Watford stock, we shall stand forever tall, facing front."

Painted tiles at the Fiesta Court, (known locally as the Campamento Festero), depicting Lady Butler's famous painting entitled "Steady the drums and fifes" This shows the 57th Regiment drawn up under fire at the ridge of Albuhera, with drummer boys in the foreground. The original is on display at The Middlesex Regiment Museum, at Dover Castle.

Picture taken at the tiled monument to the south end of the Avda Extremedura, facing traffic heading north. Paul pictured on the left with a Portuguese re-enactor in Napoleonic Cacadore uniform in the centre. The monument shows Spanish, British, French and Portuguese soldiers with the words of Lord Byron's poem about the battle in all four languages.

25

We wondered why there were so many tourists in and around the village on Albuhera Day itself, as coach-loads of people began to arrive, sporting maroon and gold ties and regimental blazers. In the scorching heat of the Spanish sun, these people were very obviously British! Our visit to the village had coincided quite by chance with an important ceremony which the Middlesex Regiment and officials from La Albuera had been planning for some time. Colonel Peter Knox explained: the colours (flags) of both the 57th and 77th Regiments were rendered obsolete in 1881, when the two regiments were combined to form The Duke of Cambridge's Own (Middlesex Regiment) and new regimental colours were designed. The old colours which had been carried into battle with each of the regiments from 1853 to 1876 (including the Crimean War of 1854/55 and the Maori War of 1863/69) were therefore put on display at St Paul's Cathedral in London, where they remained for over 120 years. During renovation works at the Cathedral in 2004, the old silk colours were taken down and found to be in such poor condition that they could not be remounted for display. A decision was then made to have the colours ceremonially buried at Albuhera (La Albuera), the scene of the regiment's finest hour and most senior battle honour. By a remarkable and happy coincidence, this special ceremony was planned for the very day Paul and I visited the village. The colours were buried at the southern elevation of the British Army monument in Wellington Park close to the banks of the Rio Albuera. The 57th West

Middlesex Regiment, the 3rd Buffs and the 2nd/31st Huntingdonshires are picked out for particular commendation and their names and insignia are inscribed on three faces of the monument. The fourth face has the name and insignia of the Princess of Wales's Royal Regiment inscribed upon it and mentions that the PWRR erected the monument in 2002. Here is a small sample of the inscription;-

57th Foot
"Die Hard 57th Die Hard"
To the immortal memory
At Albuhera we also remember and pay homage to those
brave soldiers of the Alliance - Spain and Portugal.

3rd Foot
"The Buffs"
Only 85men survived unwounded out of 728

2nd/31st Foot
Huntingdonshire (Later became) The East Surrey Regiment
"After the rest of the brigade were swept off by cavalry this little battalion alone held its ground"

The Princess Of Wales's Royal Regiment
"Oh Albuhera Glorious Field of Grief"

Brigadier Richard Holmes representing the Princess of Wales's Royal Regiment and all its forebear regiments (including the 57th) took time to read these moving words at the ceremony to bury the Middlesex Regimental Colours at the memorial in La Albuera on 16th May 2004.

For the Fallen
By Laurence Binyon 1869 – 1943

With proud thanksgiving a mother for her children, England mourns her dead across the sea. Flesh of her flesh, they were spirit of spirit, fallen for the cause of the free.

Solemn the drums thrill: Death august and royal. Songs sorrow up into immortal spheres. There is music in the midst of desolation and a glory that shines upon our tears.

They went with songs to the battle, they were young, straight of limb, true of eye, steady and aglow. They were staunch to the end against odds uncounted, they fell with their faces to the foe.

They shall not grow old as we that are left grow old, age shall not weary them nor the years condemn. At the going down of the sun and in the morning we will remember them.

They mingle not with laughing comrades again, they sit no more at familiar tables of home. They have no lot in our labour of the daytime, they sleep beyond England's foam.

But where our desires and our hopes profound, felt as a well-spring that is hidden from sight. To the innermost heart of their own land they are known, as the stars are known to the night.

As the stars that shall be bright when we are dust, moving in marches upon the heavenly plain. As the stars that are starry in the time of our darkness, to the end, to the end, they remain.

Don Manuel Diaz Gonzalez ceremonially lays the Middlesex colours to rest forever in the earth at Albuhera 16th May 2004.

Paul and I looked on along with Colonel Peter Knox and several hundred locals as well as military representatives from Britain, Spain, Portugal and France. Brigadier Richard Holmes formally handed the colours to Don Manuel Diaz Gonzalez, the Major of La Albuera for safe keeping. Don Manuel ceremonially placed the coffin containing the colours in the hallowed ground himself.

Upon our return home, local Journalist Matt Hemley wrote a detailed article for the Watford Observer newspaper about our visit and research, which was published on Friday, 16th July 2004.

Spanish Soldiers from the Badajoz Garrison pay their respects at the memorial in Wellington Park, Albuhera Day 2004.

Monument to the Spanish General Castanos who took part in the battle. This spectacle dominates the central square in La Albuera and is surrounded with flagpoles, upon which the flags of Spain, Britain, Portugal, Germany, France, Extremadura and Europe are hoisted on Albuhera Day each year.

Brigadier Richard Holmes of the Princess of Wales's Royal Regiment entrusts the Middlesex Regimental colours to The Mayor of La Albuera, Don Manuel Diaz Gonzalez. These colours which were carried by the 57th and 77th of Foot regiments from 1853 to 1876 (including their actions in the Crimea) were buried before the 57th Monument in Wellington Park at La Albuera on 16th May 2004. The monument itself was erected in May, 2001.

Members of the Middlesex Regiment and those of the 57th of Foot Re-enactment Regiment in Spain. Taken on Albuhera Day 2004. Celia Denney pictured standing with Miguel Gomez, Captain of the representative 57th Regiment in La Albuera.

Señor David Diaz, Sergeant of the 57th Company, with friends and family at Wellington Park on Albuhera Day 2004.

The 57ᵗʰ and 3ʳᵈ of Foot Spanish re-enactment companies (West Middlesex and Buffs) teeming through the village before musket drilling and re-enactment rehearsal. Excitement is mounting in the days before the fiesta.

Drummer Boys practice in the streets before the official Albuhera Day Parade. On the day they will all be in full Napoleonic uniforms. Photo taken 14th May, 2005.

Monument to commemorate the brave action and great loss suffered by Spanish and Portuguese troops at the ridge of La Albuera. The Spanish and Portuguese fought alongside the 57th of Foot on this ridge.

Albuhera Revisited.

Paul and I returned to La Albuera in May 2005, and stayed for a week at the Hostal Villafres on the Avenida de Extremadura, the main road through the village. This accommodation was comfortable, private and affordable, with a separate restaurant serving traditional Spanish food and wine - lovely. We attended the annual service at Elvas with the Friends of the British Cemetery on Saturday 14th May and had lunch with them at the Clube de Tiro e Caça

39

along with the Mayors of Elvas and La Albuera as well as the Commanders of the Portuguese and Spanish Garrisons at Elvas and Badajoz. Our friends (and possibly relations) Roger and Elaine Norris were also in attendance, and it was lovely to meet them.

That evening we returned to Albuera with Mike Ward and the other Middlesex Regulars and went on in to the heart of the village to have a look around. We spoke to a few locals carrying muskets whom we recognised from the previous year and followed them through the village to a field nearby named Wellington Park where many more were gathering. They began to practice their musket drills, marching and of course their rôles in the re-enactment, which was due to take place the following weekend. We found our friends Miguel, David and José wielding their muskets near the church in the village centre and as you would expect, we joined them again for a drink later that evening at the Campamento Festero – which they unlocked specially for us and the rest of Miguel's 57th.

The following day, Miguel collected us from our hotel and drove us to a large sparsely wooded picnic area about two miles from the village. Almost the whole village was there, about 500 people in all, for the annual village picnic. Music, singing, dancing, barbeques and games; we had a great time and got to know even more of the locals.

On Monday, the next day, we headed for the village centre early as this was the 16th May – Albuhera Day and we didn't want to miss any of the ceremonies and festivities. As it turned out, nothing was planned until about 11am, so we returned to the hotel for breakfast. When we arrived there, the restaurant and bar were crammed full of soldiers of the Spanish 16th Mechanised Regiment, who were having their own breakfast before taking part in the Albuhera Day parade. Eventually the ceremonies and festivities began and we joined many of the locals at the central square in the village for the annual formalities and speeches. From there Miguel, José and Don Manuel escorted us along with Celia Denney and other municipal and military officials to the museum nearby for a presentation and guided tour. Later, the village began to vibrate with excitement. Traditional samba floated on the breeze and the locals began to dance once again. Later, the military bands began to play and the whole place came alive. One could not help but feel the rhythm: we simply couldn't resist the temptation of dancing in the street with the locals as we made our way through the village. As we were jubilantly bounding through the streets, a Spanish television camera crew turned the corner in front of us.

The female news reporter immediately made eye contact with me and before I knew it, the camera was on me with the reporter asking me all sorts of questions in Spanish – not a nice position to be in when you don't speaka de lingo.

"I'm English, I can't speak much Spanish," I tried to explain – but to no avail. She persisted and I gathered we were live on air for the news channel which was doing a feature on the festival and the history of the village. I had very little Spanish and she had hardly any English. How embarrassing! I looked to Miguel for support. He came to my aid explaining our friendship and our family ties with La Albuera. He told her about Thomas's involvement in the battle and we were invited along with Don Manuel Diaz Gonzalez to take part in a live television interview at the Badajoz T.V. studios the following evening. We nervously agreed and then continued with the festivities, moving on to the Mayor's formal luncheon at the delightful Ventura Rosario restaurant opposite the ridge – the same venue as the lunch we attended with Colonel Peter Knox the year before. We could not count all the wonderful courses placed before us and the service was first class given the hundreds of people attending.

When we returned to our accommodation I drafted out a few words in Spanish as a kind of preparation for the television interview and tried to learn some key Spanish phrases with Paul. The following morning we did some filming of our own around the village and met our friend Domingo at one of his latest building projects with other family members.

The evening came quickly enough and Don Manuel collected us from our hotel along with Miguel. We were driven to the television studios in Badajoz, about 12 miles North West of the village. Don Manuel, Miguel and I were ushered on to the set and the interview began, completely in Spanish. Don Manuel opened with a brief history of the village and explained the importance of the battle in changing the tide of the Napoleonic Wars. He also talked about the association the Middlesex Regiment and the Princess of Wales's Royal Regiment have with the village and that Albuhera became a senior battle honour in the British Army – specifically bestowed on the 57th West Middlesex Regiment. The interviewer moved on to Miguel and asked about his involvement. He told her about his 57th re-enactment regiment in La Albuera and went on to explain how Paul and I met him in 2004 during our first visit.

After a short while the interviewer slowly turned to me and asked if I would like to say a few words. I asked if it was alright to use my Spanish notes to guide me through the things I wanted to say, which they were quite happy with and I think they rather liked the fact that I was going to at least try to speak some Spanish – so many people don't! I began…

"Buenos tardes Badajoz, ¿cõmo esta?. Soy Inglés, mi no habla mucho Español, lo siento – pero, yo probar. Mi hermano Paul y Yo, usted hemos muy muchos la amigos en La Albuera. Miguel Gomez, su famillia y su amigos. Ellos son nuestro hermanos y la hermanas Español. Nosotros amor España y nosotros amor La Albuera. El Famillia Grande. Nosotros El Famillia Grande podemos ayudar la paz en Europe. Nosotros

beber, comemos, cantamos y nosotros bailamos. Pero, de major parte, nosotros acrordase y aprender la historia de la Battala de La Albuera y el muchos muchos muerto. El Soldados Español, Portugese y Gran Bretaña, y nuestro el corazõn lleno. Viva La Famillia Grande del La Albuera, Viva España y Gran Bretaña. Viva Europe y viva El Mondo. Mi el Abuelo padre, padre, padre Thomas Norris un Soldado con el Regimento Middlesexo, el cincuenta y siete regimento Inglés. Yo escribir una libro sobre me el abuelo padre, padre, padre nombre Over The Hills and Far Away, el vide y tiempo de Thomas Norris. Publico Agosto o Septiembre este año. El dinero para la capilla San Juan en Elvas, el Inglés cemetario Napoleonique, y el dinero para la museo en La Albuera".

Roughly translated, hopefully, this means:-

"Good evening Badajoz, how are you? I'm English and I don't speak much Spanish, I'm sorry, but I will try. My brother Paul and I have very many friends in La Albuera. Miguel Gomez, his family and his friends are our brothers and sisters of Spain. We love Spain and we love the big family of La Albuera. We the Big Family together can help peace in Europe. We drink, we eat, we sing and we dance, but for the most important part, we remember and learn the history of the battle of Albuhera and the great, great loss of the Soldiers of Spain, Portugal and Great Britain, and our hearts fill. Viva the big family of Albuhera, viva Spain and Great Britain, viva Europe and viva the World. My great, great, great grandfather Thomas Norris was a soldier with the

Middlesex Regiment, the Fifty-seventh English regiment. I have written a book about him entitled Over The Hills and Far Away, the life and times of Thomas Norris. It will be published in August or September this year. Money raised will be used for work at the British Napoleonic cemetery at the Chapel of Saint John in Elvas. The money will also be used for the museum at La Albuera".

The interviewer thanked us and Don Manuel rounded off the programme, gently encouraging tourism in the region – he really is so good at his job! We went off air and made our way out to Paul who had been waiting behind the scenes. Paul had used our camcorder to capture the whole thing on tape and the studio promised to send us a DVD of the programme as it went out. We returned to La Albuera and watched a rehearsal of the annual open air play at the bullring, before making our way back to the Villafres for our last night in the village.

Miguel drove us there and when we arrived at the hotel he got out of the car with us. He hugged us as brothers do and kissed us on both checks saying in Spanish "take these kisses back to England with you and give them to your wives and children from me, your big brother in Spain". He then took our shoulders firmly and said shaking us "you are.., you are.., umm, how you say it in English?" he had to stop and asked for my phrase book to check... "Gentlemen" he finished. What greater compliment can a man be given?

Early Norris Family History

4. Early Norris Family History

The surname 'Norris' has two specific origins: the first being from the Norman family Surname 'Norreise' which was transformed in time to 'Norris' in the South East of England and 'Norice' in the North West; the second origin was 'Norhuse' from the Anglo-Saxon name for the person living in the north house, or sometimes translated as "man from the north". By the census of 1881, 'Norris' was the spelling most commonly used, with just over 12,000 people recorded with this surname in England and Wales. The Norris or 'Norreise' family of Thomas's line were originally descended from Scandinavian Vikings who settled in northern France in the 10th Century. In Scandinavia, the name Norris is associated with nursing or helping. The earliest known recorded use of the name Norreise was in 1029 near Blois at what was once a village by the same name. From Normandy the family supported Duke William (later William the Conqueror) in 1066, by providing men and horses to assist in the Norman conquest of Britain. Following the battle of Hastings William marched westward from the English coast, through the counties of Kent, Sussex and Surrey south of London, then northward to Hertfordshire. At Berkhamsted, William and his supporters built a huge mott and bailey castle as the headquarters from which the continuing conquest of Britain would be planned and managed. In the 1400's, Henry of Berkhamsted (baptised Henry Norris) was appointed Keeper of the Castle and a stone effigy of him dressed as a knight of the realm still lies alongside his wife Lady Norris in a dark corner of St Peters church in Berkhamsted. The Norris family funded the construction of the original church on its current site. Berkhamsted Castle is now in ruins, but remains a substantial structure and popular visitor attraction.

The Norris family also had a strong alliance with the wealthy and powerful Durrance or 'Durrants' family on the continent, who themselves were closely related to William. The Durrance and Norris families were rewarded for their support during the Norman Conquest and were given huge tracts of land throughout Hertfordshire, predominantly in Berkhamsted and Croxley Green. It is likely that the land was given to the Durrance family by William, and that they then passed it on to the Norris family who remained in Normandy. Eventually Sir Jean Norreise took up residency in Britain shortly after a jousting tournament at Dunstable in 1308. The coat of arms he fought under was a large black cross on a white background. The cross was in the style of the mediaeval Christian "Crux Veritas" – the cross of truth, with barbed ends. This design may have been intended to show the relationship with the Durrance family, whose coat of arms was a black coloured lion rampant facing left, surrounded by (or supported by) seven identical but smaller black crosses. Jean's sons anglicised the unpopular sounding Norman surname and in time it was written in the modern form of 'Norris' as mentioned earlier.

Their descendants remained in South Bedfordshire and West Hertfordshire, concentrating in the Tring and Berkhamsted areas by the sixteenth century. The Norris family were very wealthy and owned a good deal of farm land, brickfields and rentable dwellings in what are now Northchurch, Ashridge and Great Gaddesden. Tring Museum has some Norris-made bricks and a family bible from this period on display. In time, with the family estate gradually being divided by successive generations through inheritance and the rural exodus to London, the main property remaining in local Norris hands by the time of the industrial revolution was Norris Farm in Northchurch. The Farm House, now known as Rosemary Cottage, is still in existence on the old A41 road from Berkhamsted to Tring near the corner of New Road in Northchurch. James Norris was the last of our direct line to hold substantial property in Northchurch, which he left in trust to his young children when he died in 1755. An inventory of his possessions was drawn up upon his demise, which included six and a half hogs-heads of ale kept in his cellar. This equates to some 338 gallons or just over 2700 pints. Further records show he was the official "Chief Ale Taster" for that part of Hertfordshire and ales could only be sold to the public with his specific written approval. He clearly had a very good working relationship with the local breweries at the time.

James' wife Sarah (nee Harding) and his elder brother Henry were appointed as trustees to take care of the children and the estate, to ensure the children eventually received their inheritance once they reached the full age of twenty-one. Sadly, James' wife Sarah died the following year and his brother Henry took complete control the estate – claiming it for himself and sending James and Sarah's children off to work as live-in servants at other wealthy households throughout Hertfordshire. Henry then sold the entire estate off in lots and moved to a large property at Sopwell in St Albans, where he along with his sons later established a successful milling business.

The last member of our family to reside at the farm house was Anne Norris who sadly died there in 1818, a childless, half blind spinster, leaving the bulk of her property to her niece in London. Anne's Last Will and Testament shows she left the house and grounds stretching as far as the parcel of land she previously sold for the construction of the Grand Union Canal at the bottom of her garden. She also left her niece an unusual "God Ring" of silver and red stone, stating that it was of no monetary value, but that it was very, very precious to her. She was determined that the ring should stay in family hands and asked that her niece pass it on to her children upon her own demise.

The West Coast Main Line Railway and associated tunnels were constructed at Northchurch during the early to mid1830s, and pass directly through what was once part of Norris Farm. This is one of the busiest stretches of main line railway in Europe, linking London with Birmingham and the industrial north.

James Norris, one of James and Sarah's children, was sent to work as a servant at a house in Chipperfield. He grew up in the Rickmansworth and Watford area and eventually married a local girl by the name of Mary Evans on 27th January, 1761 at her parish Church of St James, Bushey, near Watford in Hertfordshire. They were married by the Rector James Ibbertson who presided at the church from 1748 until 1782. Shortly after their marriage, they moved to the yards (later known as 'The Watford Courts') behind the shops and taverns of the Lower High Street in Watford. This seems to have been very poor, cramped accommodation with little if any proper sanitary arrangements. It was a breeding ground for bacteria and disease. Various sources describe the locals having to wash their clothes in the River Colne at the bottom of the High Street during this period and often the only safe liquids to drink were alcoholic beverages such as gin and beer.

Not surprisingly, infant mortality was very high with only a small percentage of children surviving their first year. It is likely that this terrible fate visited James and Mary several times as the first recorded baptism for a child of theirs in Watford was for their son, also named James in 1769, some eight years after their marriage. A burial is recorded in the parish register for their daughter Mary in November the previous year. Happily though, the marriage was blessed with further healthy children; Susanna (1771), Moses (1776), David (1783) and of course Thomas* who was baptised at St Mary's Parish church, Watford High Street on 27th September, 1778 in the eighteenth year of King George III's reign. In those days birth dates were not recorded formally as this was before civil registration was introduced in Britain. It was the Christian duty of all parents to ensure their children were baptised within two weeks of their birth or by the next Saints Day. Failure to comply with this requirement would result in a monetary fine of around a week's wages payable to the church. In addition, religion was taken very literally in those days and parents would have been keen to have their children baptised as early as possible in order to ensure divine protection.

This is where our story of Thomas's extraordinary life begins.

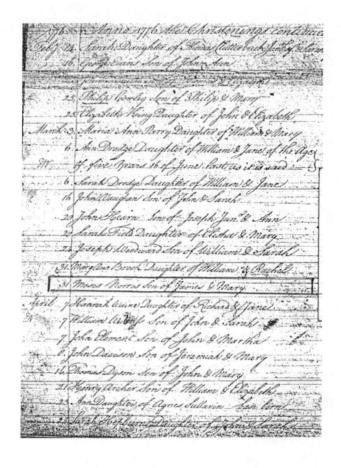

St Mary's Parish Church Register. Baptism record for Moses Norris, son of James and Mary dated 31st March 1776

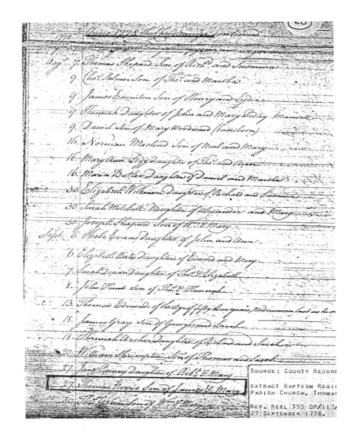

St Mary's Parish Church Register. Baptism record for Thomas Norris Son of James and Mary dated 27th September 1778.

St Mary's Parish Church Register. Burial of Moses son of James and Mary Norris recorded 21st January 1799.

The Life and Times of Thomas Norris

5. The Life and Times of Thomas Norris

We can say with some confidence that Thomas was born in the second or third week of September 1778. Somehow Thomas and his siblings survived the appalling domestic conditions and eventually against all odds reached adulthood. Many of their childhood haunts would have been in common with some of those enjoyed by myself and my own brothers during the 1970's when we lived in West Watford. Places like The Rookery, Cassiobury Park and the River Colne are still very popular today. Sadly we find a burial record for Thomas's elder brother "Moses – son of James & Mary Norris" in Watford St Mary's Parish Church register dated 21st January, 1799. As usual, no cause of death is given, although he would have been 22 years of age, having been born in March 1776.

Imprisonment

Thomas, who worked as a butcher in Watford at the time, must have been greatly affected by this loss as the family appears to have entered a period of even greater turmoil and hardship, which eventually in 1801 landed Thomas in court at St Albans. He was accused of stealing two loaves of bread from a bakers shop on Watford High Street. At the age of almost twenty-three, Thomas was found guilty of this very serious crime and was to be severely punished for it. He was sentenced to seven years hard labour in the colonies with a recommendation of transportation to Australia. Thomas was taken down to a hulk – a prison ship on the Thames in London to await transit. The conditions there must have been unbearable as records show only a small percentage of those entering the prison ships actually survived long enough to be transported.

After a few weeks, Thomas somehow managed to escape captivity and made his way up river as far as Henley-On-Thames, avoiding detection by the authorities who were no doubt in hot pursuit. During his time in Henley-On-Thames, Thomas met a young lady by the name of Ann Buck, who was from a respectable and relatively well to do local family. After a short time they decided to get married and arrangements were made to publish the banns at their respective parish churches.

The purpose of this is to advertise the fact that the marriage is planned and to provide the opportunity for any objections to be raised before or during the marriage ceremony. For example, if Thomas already had a wife and children in Watford, publishing the banns would allow the church in Watford to advise the Church in Henley-On-Thames that Thomas was already married – it would also give any previously abandoned spouse the opportunity of claiming financial support for herself and any children.

Thomas must have been hoping to put his colourful history behind him and looking forward to starting a new life with a clean slate in Henley-On-Thames. Unfortunately for him, he had not realised the significance of the banns being published in his own parish of Watford St Mary's and before long the authorities in Watford caught on to the location of the prison ship escapee. At the age of twenty-four, Thomas married Ann Buck on 18th October, 1802 at her parish church of St Mary the Virgin in Henley-On-Thames. But with Thomas now being such an easy target, the authorities arrived in Henley-On-Thames a short time after the wedding. Little was he to know the fate that awaited him.

War with France

At the time, Britain faced an increasing and very real military threat from revolutionary France under the leadership of Napoleon Bonaparte. Napoleon's military successes on the continent had bred huge confidence in France where a new kind of nationalism was being embraced following the brutal demise of their monarchy. By 1806, the French army had swept aside any kind of resistance put up by their neighbouring countries and with his unprecedented success at the Battle of Austerlitz where the French were outnumbered two to one against a combined force of Russians and Prussians, Napoleon became master of Europe. To resist French attempts to dominate Europe and to protect Southern England and the more remote British colonies from invasion, Britain needed to recruit soldiers quickly to form a large, well trained standing army.

With the constant threat of war, it was extremely difficult to recruit volunteers and so it was decided that convicted criminals would be offered the opportunity of paying their debt to society by joining the army instead of serving out their prescribed sentences in prisons. Many prisoners took up the offer hoping the threat of war would pass before the end of their sentences. Thomas was among them and he joined the 1st Battalion of the 57th Regiment of foot infantry, otherwise known as the West Middlesex Regiment on 16th December, 1803.

Army Recruitment

Imagine you lived in England about two hundred years ago. Common people live like animals and are only concerned with obtaining money in order to pay for food to stay alive. Life is harsh, you can trust no one. You are a single independent man of about twenty-five years of age and you are standing in a town square or main high street outside a tavern. You have not eaten for a day or two and what you do normally get to eat is tasteless and barely fit for human consumption. There's never much of anything to eat and you can't remember the last time you ate meat as it's so expensive – if you steal food or livestock it is likely you will be imprisoned, flogged or hanged.

You live in a damp hovel at the back of the high street with no means of heating or sanitation. There is no social security or National Health Service. Hospitals are not available to the public and most of the drugs we now rely on have not yet been invented. The butchers and tanners yards are nearby so the pavements are covered in animal blood and tannin which is swept out of the yards and into your direct neighbourhood with buckets of filthy water. You dare not complain about this, as the yard owners are wealthy and pay thugs to keep the local population at bay.

In any case, these are normal domestic conditions. The whole area stinks and disease is rife. You can only cook from an open fire, but firewood is expensive too, so you can't afford to cook for yourself either. You must pay for everything and you own nothing. You are employed as a farm labourer, with long hours but very low pay – so much so that you return home from work exhausted and starving every evening.

Most of your pay goes to the landlord as rent for your hovel – if you don't pay it you will be beaten or maybe flogged as a debtor and thrown out on the streets. It is illegal to live on the streets and the authorities would punish you again. You have no access to clean water and the only available safe liquid to drink is either gin or ale, which you must buy from one of the taverns. Gin is much cheaper than ale, but you only get a small shot. Obviously you have to eat and drink to stay alive and so the local taverns take what remains of your pay in return for bread and gin. Your money will only last you a maximum of four or five days per week provided you stick to very basic food and little gin. If you eat meat, you will only have two or three meals in the whole week.

The authorities are very imposing and there is little to be had in the way of freedom. Education is not available to you so you are unable to read, write or even manage the most basic arithmetic. To the wealthier people in town you are scum, regarded as a beast of the field – not even the same species.

But you are a good person and try to keep faith with the moral and ethical teachings of the bible – you attend church regularly, although the services are all given in Latin so you can't understand them. The church is corrupt as are most of the politicians and those of any social standing in the town. You are not eligible to vote because you are poor. Honesty and decency are seen as weakness; greed and brutality are admired.

You are clothed in filthy rags which you work and sleep in, only taking time once a week or so to wash in a local river which is also used to power a local silk mill and provides contaminated water for beer making. You would be very lucky to have boots or shoes. Standing there, you watch a band of army recruiters march smartly in to the town square and begin their recruitment pitch. Once a crowd has gathered, the Sergeant Major leads with ribbons streaming from his shako (hat) and with the regimental colours flying he announces loudly.......

"Hear Ye, hear Ye, hear Ye. Let no man here tell me that he has had no dinner, for I count that to be a fool's cry – as would any officer or soldier of the gallant 57th of foot, the West Middlesex Regiment, with company regimentals you see I am". Pointing to his accompanying men and the regimental colours to show his official capacity in recruitment. *"No man that I ever signed up for glory ever wants for his grub".* Holding up a shilling he says, *"Once this shining coin is taken, a bargain is struck between you and me, for as his Majesty and thee. Bread, six pound at once! And while you're with me, all the ale you can drink. I turn off the tap never, in my company it is a constant amber flow. Watch the air fill with gold, lads".* The Sergeant slowly empties a handful of golden coins into his tipped shako one by one whilst the crowd are astounded to see so much money falling through the air. He continues to explain, *"what's called bounty"* and tells them how much it is. *"which can not include this"* holding up another shilling he says " *for this is a gift from His Majesty himself, who said to me – Sergeant go and find me lads and they'll fight for me and catch me eagles as my heroes"* referring to the French eagle standards which head their infantry columns.

Pointing to one of the taverns in the high street he says, *"Come inside that I may feed my lambs and give them spirits, and he who wishes may join. Come on lads, there's ale a plenty. I turns off the tap never."* Half starved you follow him into the tavern along with a handful of others to eat and drink to your hearts' content. Once well fed and "watered", you agree to join the army by taking the King's Shilling and signing your illiterate 'X' mark on the recruitment papers to make this a legally binding contract. You are no longer a free man; however, you will be given two square meals a day (breakfast and dinner), a full suit of clothes to keep you warm and possibly for the first time in your life, a good pair of boots to wear. Given that Britain was almost constantly at war with France for some 22 years between 1793 and 1815, recruitment posts sprang up in every town and they became as common as post offices are nowadays.

As we have already mentioned, Thomas joined the 57th Regiment on 16th December, 1803. He did this using his deceased brother's name "Moses" for one of two possible reasons. Firstly, and most likely, is that he was trying to evade detection by the authorities, who by now knew where he was. Sufficient time had passed for them to have caught up with him in either Henley or Watford and he would have been looking for a means of escape. Had he been caught, he would have expected to face transportation to Australia following a brutal beating. The second possibility is that he may have been given the opportunity of serving out his sentence in the army as many other convicts did at the time – although this does not explain the change of Christian name. We will explore the evidence to support this theory in greater detail later in this book and there is no need for the subject to detain us here. The fact that Thomas Norris used the name Moses when he joined the army is a certainty.

Upon entering the army each new recruit had to undergo a basic physical examination by the regimental surgeon to prove their fitness to serve. This was to prevent the spread of any existing illness or diseases among the men and to make sure they were all physically capable of carrying out the normal duties associated with soldiering. Generally, if they had two arms and two legs they were in, as the surgeons often succumbed to bribes from officers trying to meet their recruitment quotas. At this point a record was made of their physical features. This was to ensure that those queuing to receive their periodic army pay actually fitted the description of the person they were claiming to be thus preventing false payments. Thomas was recorded as being 5'8½" tall with brown hair, grey eyes and a dark complexion, which apart from the dark complexion is close to a description of my own father – well, perhaps when he has been in the sun! Generally these physical descriptions are based on the allocation of characteristics given as one of five basic standard categories:-

Hair – Brown, Grey, Black, Red or Blonde.

Eyes   – Brown, Grey, Green, Blue or Hazel.
Complexion   – Fair, Sallow, Dark, Fresh or Ruddy.

Various trades descriptions in Thomas's regiment included: Butchers, Gilders, Upholsterers, Labourers and Sawyers.

The new recruits were initially provided with white coloured uniforms comprising a pair of trousers, a jacket, a cap, a black collar stock, black boots and gaiters. These were worn during the early weeks of basic training before proper uniforms and muskets were issued. Thomas was allocated to the 4th Company of the 1st Battalion, which as far as we can tell, was a centre line company as opposed to a flank or light infantry company.

57th of Foot Uniform

Once the new recruits had completed their basic training, they were issued with a full uniform, the design of which was unique to each particular regiment. The 57th uniform comprised a standard design infantry tunic or "coatee" made of brick red coloured wool, with yellow facings added (collars and cuffs). The coatee also had a special white lacing about ½" wide, with a single black line weaved through its centre. This was sewn horizontally across the chest section in five pairs of rectangles and vertically down the cuffs, again in pairs. These 'lacings' were purely decorative and all of a square-ended design – the lace itself being similar to that of wide modern boot laces. Officer's uniform lacing was gold. The buttons on the coatee front and cuffs bore the number 57 and this along with the unique combination of yellow facing colour and white square-ended double spaced lacings with a single black line clearly identified anyone wearing it as a member of the West Middlesex Regiment. Drummer's coatees were made more decoratively, in the colour of the regimental facing, in this case yellow, rather than brick red. The men were also given white coloured wool or canvass trousers and a black 'stove pipe'-type shako. The 7" tall shako head dress was mounted centrally with a white over red plume at the top, and had a standard George III brass shako plate fixed to the front. The shako plate had the royal cipher with a crown, crossed weapons and lion embossed upon it. Beyond this, the soldiers were given a leather bayonet baldrick (sling) and black leather ammunition box, along with white leather belts to suspend these from their shoulders to the opposite sides of their bodies. The white belts were worn with the ammunition box on the right side of the body and the bayonet on the left – thus the white belts crossed each other at the centre of the chest. Special metal regimental belt plates were worn where these white belts crossed at the front, although, perhaps unexpectedly, the belts were not connected by these plates. The reason for this is one of safety – if the ammunition box caught fire it needed to be removed quickly away from the body.

In the case of the 57th, the belt plate design was a heavy cast highly polished brass oval, depicting three swords within a shield above the number 57, surrounded by an ornate sword belt and buckle with the words "West Middlesex Regiment". A crown finishes off the design, mounted above the swords and belt. (See National Army Museum display piece 9006-5 in the Waterloo Rooms, which is a bi-metal officer's version). The later design (from 1816 onwards) was rectangular with the number 57 surrounded by laurels tied with ribbon and surmounted with a crown. Again this was a heavy cast of metal but with dimensions of about 3" x 3½". Interestingly, the regimental uniform colours of yellow, red and black are also the colours of Watford Football Club, known in the UK as "The Hornets".

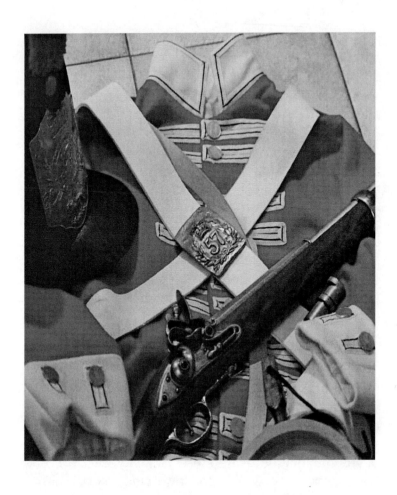

Replica 57th of Foot uniform produced by Nancy Dench of The Sutlers Stores in Bournemouth. Brown Bess musket also from The Sutlers Stores and 57th belt plate supplied by Ronald Bridgehouse. Kitty Hats of North Wycombe made the Stovepipe Shako.

Now they were given their muskets – the famous India pattern Brown Bess musket, which stood over 6ft 3" tall with its 18" bayonet fitted. Over a million of these were issued through the Napoleonic period and it remained the preferred weapon of the British Army for many years after. The men were also provided with light canvas bread bags to carry provisions, and round wooden water canisters painted sky blue – the colour of water. Each man would mark the number of his regiment, battalion and company on his water canister in either white paint or chalk along with a white arrow pointing upward to the outlet and hardwood stopper. The canister was suspended by a long brown leather belt, about an inch or so wide, which was slung over the right shoulder to carry it on the left side of the body for ease of access.

Much of the money, the 'bounty' that each new recruit had been given for joining the army was spent paying for their uniforms and for what were termed as 'necessaries' like soap, boot polish, lace, pipe clay and tea. For example, in 1812 bounty payments including the King's Shilling amounted to two pounds and twelve shillings. Once all payments had been made to the army for uniforms and necessaries, only 10 shillings were left – but this was still a substantial amount of money to the common man. Costs for necessaries were automatically deducted from regular army pay – whether you were given them or not. It is unlikely that Thomas was given any kind of home leave during his military career and he would not have heard of his father James' death in 1807 until he returned to England several years later.

Under some circumstances though, married quarters were provided with little more than a blanket thrown over a tightened rope to separate couples. In Thomas's case, Ann probably did not join her husband until after 1815. Napoleon's constant threat and undying determination to rule Europe meant that Britain could ill-afford for its troops to abscond while on leave, and so except for officers, the opportunity for this was in most cases removed. As many as one in ten wives were allowed to follow the army with their children, provided they cooked and laundered.

An unique scaled model of Thomas Norris made for the author by Napoleonic modelling expert Stephen Voller of Watford in 1996. The shako and trousers are of the design issued to the regiment in 1812. This head dress is known as the "Waterloo Shako" design.

Over the Hills and Far Away

Here are the words to a commonly sung infantry song from Thomas's time in the Iberian Peninsula Campaign. Some of the words are very familiar to most of us as they harp back to childhood nursery rhymes. Little did I know then, that the theme had come from the Napoleonic Wars:-

"Here's fourteen shillings on the drum, for those who'll volunteer to come,
To list and fight the foe today, over the hills and far away.

[chorus:]Over the hills and over the main, through Flanders Portugal and Spain, King George commands and we obey, over the hills and far away.

Through smoke and fire and shot and shell, unto the very walls of hell,
We shall stand and we shall stay, over the hills and far away.

[chorus]

Now though I travel far from Spain, a part of me shall still remain,
For you are with me night and day, over the hills and far away.

[chorus]

So fall in lads behind the drum, with colours blazing like the sun,
Along the road and come-what-may, over the hills and far away.

[chorus]

When evil stalks upon the land, I'll neither hold nor stay my hand,
But fight to win a better day, over the hills and far away.

[chorus]

If I should fall to rise no more, as many comrades did before,
Ask the pipes and drums to play, over the hills and far away.

[chorus]

Let kings and Tyrants come and go, I'll stand ajudged by what I know,
A soldier's life I'll never again say, over the hills and far away.

[chorus]"

Thomas spent about four months training with the regiment then known as the "Steel Backs" (due to their regular floggings) in England, then in April, 1804 he was sent to the Channel Island of Guernsey. This period saw a massive build up of British forces on the Channel Islands, in preparation for an anticipated French invasion. Eventually the immediate invasion threat passed and in November 1804, Thomas and his regiment were posted to Gibraltar.

At the time Gibraltar was a pivotal military base which controlled all trade and military movements between Africa, America and the rich Mediterranean countries. Britain's Naval supremacy had long been established and with a large, well built and well manned fleet, Britain was able to dominate international waters almost unhindered. Gibraltar was continuously supplied with food and men via the sea trading routes, which were protected by the Royal Navy. This helped Britain to maintain a firm hold on the region. Failure to supply the garrison and fleet at Gibraltar by sea would mean giving up the base and consequently would reduce Britain's power and standing on the world stage. The British navy was tested during Thomas's stay at Gibraltar, when in 1805, Horatio Nelson settled things once and for all off cape Trafalgar.

Unfortunately, Lord Nelson was killed in the courageous action and his name, along with that of his flag ship "Victory" were added indelibly to our list of national heroes. Had Nelson failed at Trafalgar, the combined Spanish and French armada would have headed directly for Gibraltar and slaughtered the garrison – including Thomas who was stationed there at the time. In addition, Britain would have lost its control of the seas and ultimately Napoleon Bonaparte would have invaded Britain with little resistance. By now we would all be speaking French and our own native language would have gone the way of Latin, consigned to text books and religious artwork. Fortunately for us and for Thomas, this was not to be.

In an attempt to weaken the British in preparation for his planned invasion of southern England, Napoleon imposed an economic blockade throughout continental Europe to prevent any country from trading across the English Channel. The Portuguese refused to take part despite serious military threats from the French, and in time, Napoleon invaded Portugal. This was done with initial backing from Spain, who allowed French forces safe passage through their country to Portugal. In retaliation, the British government also imposed an embargo in 1807, banning all trade between France and Britain, including British colonies and their remaining allies throughout the world. This was extended to include a ban on American trade with France and this eventually led to the British war with the United States a few years later. Napoleon's deal with Spain was to occupy Portugal and divide it into French and Spanish provinces – effectively carving it up for themselves. Napoleon gradually filled Spain with his troops too and in time took control of the entire Iberian Peninsula. By March 1808, Napoleon had some 100,000 men in Spain and seized Madrid itself. With the Spanish now suffering the same fate as the Portuguese, Napoleon had no reason to keep to his bargain. The Spanish monarchy went into exile and Napoleon installed his own brother Joseph as King of Spain.

The French now had control on land and the British had control over the sea. Spain and Portugal along with most of the other European powers had all but yielded to the French and if Britain remained inactive on land abroad, Napoleon would strike at England herself. Britain needed to force attention away from her own coasts and to rally pro-British support on the continent. To do this and to relieve the suffering of Portugal and Spain, Britain decided to deploy troops in Iberia. Control of the sea meant they could supply their moving army with provisions from any of the ports on the Atlantic, Mediterranean or Channel coasts, to help force the French eastward out of Iberia. And so began the Peninsula War, known to the Spanish as their War of Independence.

The major part of any remaining Spanish military resistance was almost overcome by the invading French. The local populations quickly formed separate territorial style regional armies but were ill-equipped and largely untrained. They also had no overall command or combined strategy.

Notwithstanding this, at first they managed to force much of the French army into retreat and at one point Napoleon's brother Joseph was forced out of Madrid leaving most of Spain unoccupied. This caused the French forces under the command of General Junot in Portugal to be cut off from the rest of their army leaving them in a vulnerable position. Without supplies, communications or a safe means of retreat out of Portugal and through Spain to France, they were left to sit and wait several months for reinforcements to arrive. This timing coincided perfectly with the initial British intervention in Iberia. The First British expedition to the Peninsula (which did not involve the 57th regiment) arrived in early August 1808, under the initial command of Sir Arthur Wellesley. They successfully took on Junot's French forces at Rolica and Vimiero before Wellesley's superior commanding officers arrived – these being Lieutenant-Generals Sir Hew Dalrymple, Sir Harry Burrard and the famous Sir John Moore. Sir Hew negotiated a French surrender with Junot, which not only allowed the French troops safe passage home, but also included the use of British ships to transport them back to France along with all their artillery, ammunition, food and stores. Although this arrangement did rid Portugal of all French forces, the degree of leniency raised several eyebrows back in England and all three senior men were recalled with Wellesley to face an inquiry. Only Wellesley emerged from this unscathed but was returned to his previous political duties in Dublin as Chief Secretary of Ireland. Note that Sir Hew Dalrymple went on to become

Colonel of the West Middlesex Regiment in 1811 and eventually signed Thomas Norris's discharge papers in 1816 – we have a copy of his signature on file.

Sir John Moore was given orders to return to the Peninsula to aid the remaining Spanish armies in pushing the French from Spain too. Moore marched his army into central Spain but found it difficult to convince the Spanish Generals to collaborate with him as allies. Napoleon, frustrated at the recent turn of events in Spain now brought 125,000 troops to Madrid intent on crushing the Spanish and British armies in one fell swoop. Moore was reluctant to retreat in the face of this massive force, but had little choice. The British then marched several hundred miles through the mountains in freezing conditions during Christmas week, back to the coastal city of Corunna with the French in hot pursuit. Eventually the British were shipped from Corunna back to England after a final gallant defence of the port, in which Sir John Moore was killed. The British still maintained a small force at Lisbon, which had been largely ignored by the French. This small base was quietly fortified over time and provided a secure gateway for future British forces arriving in the Peninsula for years to come. Britain was not beaten yet and another task force with a new Commander in Chief was soon to be on its way.

Arthur Wellesley was given the 57th of foot during his second posting to the Iberian Peninsula to push Napoleon's Grande Armie now under the command of Marshall Soult out of Portugal. He succeeded in doing this within a month or two of arriving in Lisbon in April 1809, and following his overwhelming victory at the battle of Talavera, he was given a peerage, taking the title Viscount Wellington. This was a hard life for common soldiers, particularly in Thomas's early days in the Peninsula as the army and its camp followers were not provided with tents until 1812. They slept in the open or in makeshift bivouacs if no other form of shelter was available. During the colder winter months the armies generally went in to special winter quarters and both sides abstained from fighting and lengthy marches.

Thomas Norris landed with the 57th at Lisbon, Portugal on 15th July, 1809 and after a fortnight travelled inland by boat along the River Tagus as far as Vellada. From there the regiment marched approximately 170 kilometres through Santarem, Abrantes, Nisa and Castel Branco eventually arriving in Zarza la Major on 14th August where it joined British forces under Marshal Beresford. Almost immediately, the British force had to retreat back to Nisa and the 57th then joined the 2nd brigade of General Hill's 2nd Division at Elvas near the Portuguese boarder with Spain on 7th September.

In early December the bulk of the British forces moved north but the 57th remaining under General Hill were left to watch the French, who were occupying ground between the rivers Tagus and Guardiana. This kept the 57th busy for most of 1810.

In September 1810 though, the French under Reynier, whom Thomas's regiment had been keeping under surveillance moved to concentrate their forces with those under Massena in the north and attempted a determined mass attack into Portugal at Bussaco. The 57th along with the rest of Hill's division marched north to join Wellington's main army which it did on the eve of battle. Although the 57th remained out of French sight and did not actually come into action at the battle of Bussaco on 26th and 27th September 1810, their presence as part of Hill's 2nd division prevented the French turning the British during continued attacks to the British centre and thus prevented the French from making ground. The French were unsuccessful and decided to take a more northerly route into Portugal while the smaller British force under Wellington began to retreat to the famous defensive "Lines of Torres Vedras" which had been in preparation for some time.

The 57th marched through Espinhal, Thomar and Villafranca to Alhandra, a tactical position on the river Tagus where they arrived on 11th October, 1810. They watched the French as they took up a strong position in the Zezere valley, and in doing so the 57th as part of the 2nd division separated itself from the main British army. The main British army carefully retreated to Torres Vedras which was heavily defended with all manner of fortifications and obstacles in an attempt to lure the French to fight at a disadvantage. The French remained in the valley for around three months but found it impossible to penetrate the Lines of Torres Vedras. Eventually, the French were starved out and began to retreat. The British had well established supply lines from the coast supported by the Royal Navy, whereas the French as usual had to live off the land.

This was ultimately the great blunder of Napoleon's overall strategy as not only were his troops poorly fed, but what they did eat was stolen from the local Portuguese and Spanish population. This only served to fuel local anti-French tendencies, so when Napoleon had his own brother Joseph crowned King of Spain, much of the general populous entered into guerrilla warfare supporting the British. Wellington's strict policy was that any food taken from the local population must be properly obtained and fairly paid for, and this gained much respect throughout the Iberian Peninsula. Napoleon's smash-and-grab tactics by contrast allowed him to deploy troops very quickly, but often caused heavy losses due to starvation, illness and fatigue – the most horrific example of this being the loss of his troops to starvation during the freezing winter march on Moscow.

All this time, the 57th had remained East of the French and moved to a more strategic position north-east of Alhandra at Chamusca on the river Tagus. During the French retreat, the 57th initially joined in an effort to chase them out of Portugal, but when Wellington was sure the French would not fight and that they had begun their final retreat in early March 1811, he ordered the British 2nd division, including the 57th (now under Marshal Beresford as General Hill had temporarily returned to England) to march with his entire army to the strategic fortress stronghold of Badajoz, just over the Spanish boarder. The allied Spanish garrison there was by this time under siege by another French force under Marshal Soult. Before the 2nd division could concentrate their forces in response as planned at Portalgre, the Spanish had already surrendered Badajoz on 11th March. The British 2nd division was then ordered to advance urgently to Campo Major in a direct route to Badajoz. When the British continued their southeastern march from there, toward Badajoz, the almost obsolete fortress of Campo Major, now behind them, was attacked by the French under Mortier and after a gallant defence, Campo Major also surrendered to the French early on 25th March.

Word of this quickly reached the British en route to Badajoz, and a decision was made to return to Campo Mayor immediately. The British recaptured Campo Mayor from the French that evening, along with substantial food and ammunition stores which had been brought there earlier that day by the French. This was most fortunate as the supply lines could be very unreliable and often troops went for days without food and clean water. Little was available in the way of clothing or footwear, so life was pretty hard. Any comfort provided by the British recovery of Campo Major must have been a great relief to private soldiers like Thomas. The French withdrew beyond the river Guardiana, nearer to Badajoz. The British essentially followed, but went via Elvas just over the Portuguese border, then south, then east crossing the Guardiana at Jerumenha where the river narrows, in order to approach Badajoz from the South. A bridge had to be constructed at Jerumenha to facilitate this route, which, due to lack of materials led to a delay of about a week. British troops crossed the new bridge on 6th April and began their eastward march.

The medieval city of Badajoz stands on the river Guardiana with an ornate entrance bridge with white stone towers on the approach from the north. This was once guarded by the almost impenetrable fortress of San Christobal. Approaching Badajoz from the south as the British planned avoids crossing a river during an assault on the city. It also avoids the fortress artillery until the main city is taken and forces the enemy's back to a wide, un-fordable river – encouraging them to flee the city itself thus affording some shelter for the British troops.

By 11th April, the 2nd division including the 57th of foot had arrived at Albuera, a small village located around twelve miles southeast of the provincial capital city of Badajoz on the main North/South road now known as the "Avenida De Extremadura". Before the advance on Badajoz could commence, the British had to wait three weeks for siege equipment and artillery to arrive as they were so ill-prepared for this turn of events. A small number of very old and antique cannons were amassed, with some being over two hundred years old – which was the best the Portuguese could provide by this time. Wellington visited the army to view the defences at Badajoz, and directed Marshal Beresford to begin the siege immediately. Wellington was sure that the French Marshal Soult would bring his substantial army known to be at Cadiz in the south to relieve Badajoz from the British siege. In order to prevent this happening, the British would have to force a battle remote from Badajoz to protect the siege and either delay or stop an enemy advance. After careful consideration, Wellington and Beresford agreed that the most advantageous place to fight would be at a natural ridge close to the remote village of La Albuera.

Albuera or Albuhera as the British called it, was ideally situated as it lay to the south between the French army and Badajoz and gave the British time to prepare as they already held the ground. The French would have to come to them. On 6th May, the British began the siege of Badajoz in earnest, making their main attack at the fort of San Christobal on the north side of the city – somewhat unwisely, as this was the best defended aspect. The old Portuguese cannons proved to be inadequate for the task as the fortress of San Christobal is set very high on the north bank of the river Guardiana, with extremely tall sheer stone walls built on a base of bedrock.

In my own experience during a visit to Badajoz in May 2004, it is difficult enough to even walk from the foot of the hill to the fortress walls let alone fight your way there or carry up siege equipment. Immensely powerful cannon would have been needed to make any kind of dent in the lofty defences of San Christobal, given the line, elevation and distance of artillery fire involved. Little more had been achieved by 12th May when news came that the French under Marshal Soult were advancing as expected with an army in excess of 23,000 men from Cadiz. Beresford immediately arranged to meet the Spanish Generals, Castanos and Ballasteros along with Blake at La Albuera to form an allied army large enough to hold off this huge French force and thus prevent the relief of Badajoz.

The Battle of Albuera 16th May, 1811

The site of the battlefield at Albuera is a series of shallow undulating hills which fall more sharply as they reach a stream which runs through the lower part of the village. Nowadays – probably as then, the land is used for agricultural farming and large sways of the ridge are given over to olive groves. This is where Beresford assembled an allied army of around 15,000 men on 15th May, 1811, having left the 4th Division at Badajoz to continue the siege until as late as possible. Blake joined Beresford late at night and General Cole along with the British 4th Division and a Spanish brigade were expected from Badajoz at dawn.

Forces at Albuera in 1811

The British Army

The British Army under Field Marshal Sir William Carr Beresford was split into three distinct divisions headed by Major-General Stewart, Major-General Galbraith Lowry Cole and Brigadier-General Sir William Lumley. Brigades were arranged as set out below:-

Division	Brigade	Regiment	Strength
STEWART:	Colborne	1st Batt/ 3rd Foot (Buffs)	755
	(E.Surreys)	2nd Batt/31st Foot	418
	(Nptons)	2nd Batt/48th Foot	452
	(Berks)	2nd Batt/66th Foot	441
	Hoghton	29th Foot (Worcs)	507
	(Nptons)	1st Batt/48th Foot	497
		1st Batt/57th Foot	**647**
	Abercrombie	28th Foot (Gloucs)	519
	(Borders)	2nd Batt /34th Foot	596
	(Dorsets)	2nd Batt/39th Foot	482
COLE:	Myer	1stBatt/7th Royal Fusiliers	714
		2nd Batt/7th Royal Fusiliers	568
		1st Batt/23rd Welsh Fusiliers	733
	Von Alten	1st Batt/ Kings German Legion	588

		2nd Batt/ Kings German Legion	510
LUMLEY:	De Grey	3rd Dragoon Guards (4 squadrons)	374
		4th Dragoon Guards (4 squadrons)	387
		13th Light Dragoons (4 squadrons)	403
ARTILLERY:	Major Hawker		6no 9LB cannon
	Captain Lefeyre		4no 6LB cannon & Horse Artillery.

Infantry units were equipped with India Pattern Brown Bess muskets. The Welsh Fusiliers had 'Newland' pattern muskets and the Kings German Legion along with the 3rd & 13th Dragoons had 'Tower' muskets or carbines. The 4th Dragoons carried 'Paget' muskets and the Portuguese Rifle companies used 'Bakers' rifles similar to those normally used by the British Rifles regiments such as the 95th Green Jackets of Richard Sharpe fame.

All cavalry regiments (the dragoons) were also equipped with swords for use in close fighting. Field Marshall Beresford's uniform consisted of a navy blue double breasted knee-length tunic with ornate navy blue braiding the full length of the chest section. He would have worn a red sash around his waist with a white sword belt and black scabbard. His trousers would have been sky blue and worn over black riding boots. His headdress was a black half moon shape known as a bicorne, worn to point forward, or as described at the time, worn "fore and aft". The headdress cockade was a white over red plume of cut feathers, held in place with a navy blue fan at its base. Generally, the British infantry were dressed in red coats and the French wore blue. However, many of the British artillery units wore blue uniforms, which could be mistaken for French uniforms in the thick of battle and this lead to considerable confusion at times. The British rifle regiments wore dark green uniforms.

The Spanish Army (under Capitan Javier Castanos)

Division	Brigade	Regiment	Strength
BLAKE	J. Cansinos	Murcia Regiment	696
		Canaries Regiment	661
	C.G. Cansinos	1st Batt/ Leon Regiment	372
		Campo Mayor Regiment	731
BALLESTEROS	C.Gouvea-Asensio	1st Batt/ Catalonia Regiment	518
		Bartastro Regiment	654
		Pravia Regiment	607

	E. Carvajal	Lena Regiment	624
		Castropol Regiment	720
		1st Batt/Cangas de Tineo Reg't	303
		Infiesto Regiment	665
ZAYAS	S. Molina	2nd Batt/ Spanish Guards	585
		4th Batt/ Spanish Guards	662
		Walona Guards	676
	T. Inglesias	Irlanda Regiment	670
		The Extranjera Legion	715
	J. Fernandez	Toledo Regiment	685
		Patria Regiment	646
		Cuidad Rodrigo Regiment	597
LOY	Alvares-Almieda	Santiago Regiment	298
		Castilla Hussars	407
	C. Aviles	Mounted Grenadiers	298
	C.Espana	Regiment de Rey	630
		Regiment de la Reina	598
		Navarra Volunteers	493
	P. Villemuir	The Loyola-Este cavalry	403

		The Carjavol cavalry	319
ARTILLERY	J. De Miranda	The Alaman Battery	164
		The Villanueva Battery	158 With 4 x 6Lb cannon.

The Spanish units were generally equipped with the Spanish Hontoria muskets with bayonets fitted. General Castanos' uniform is described as a white double breasted tailed coatee with navy blue cuffs and trims. He would have worn a red sash around his waist and over his right shoulder. His gilt sword in its white scabbard was suspended by fine gilt chains from a white leather belt around his waist. His white bicorne head dress was trimmed with gold braiding and shortly cut white feathers along the length of its upper circumference, worn fore and aft to point forward. His trousers were also white, and these would have been tucked into the tops of his black riding boots, which were finished with an inverted "v" at the knee, pointing upwards.

The Portuguese Army

Brigadier General A. Luiz Fonseca	2nd Infantry Regiment		
	9th Infantry Regiment		
	10th Infantry Regiment		

	14th Infantry Regiment		
	The Lusitania Regiment.		
Colonel Collins	5th Infantry Regiment		
	5th Carcadores		
	60th Portuguese Fusiliers		
ARTILLERY	Major Braune & Captain Arriaga	6no 9LB cannon	
		6no 6LB cannon	

The French Army

The French Army under Marshal Jean De Dieu Soult (from 1807 the Duke of Dalmatia) was split into four divisions headed by; Brigadier-General Jean-Baptiste Girard, Major-General Honore Gazan, Major-General Francois Saint-Exubry and General Charles Marie Latour-Maubourg. The various brigades were arranged as follows:-

Division	*Brigade*	*Regiment*	*Strength*
GIRARD	D. Gereaux	34th Line Infantry	953
		40th Line Infantry	813

	De Le Compte	1st 2nd & 3rd Batt/ 64th Line Infantry	1529
		88th Line Infantry	899
GAZAN	A. Rochefort	21st Line Infantry	788
		1st 2nd & 3rd Batt/ 28th Line Infantry	1414
	A.Blum	100th Line Infantry	732
		1st 2nd & 3rd Bat/103rd Line Infantry	1290
ST-EXUBRY	F.Werle	1st 2nd & 3rd Batt/12th Line Infantry	2198
		1st 2nd & 3rd Batt/55th Line Infantry	1842
		1st 2nd & 3rd Batt/58th Line Infantry	1630
LATOUR	J.Briche	2nd Hussars Regt (4 squadrons)	305
MAUBOURG		10th Hussars Regt (4 squadrons)	265
		21st Cacadores	256
	B. des Eclat	14th Dragoons (4 squadrons)	406
		20th Dragoons (4 squadrons)	266
		26th Dragoons (4 squadrons)	249

	R.Murat	21st Cacadores (4 squadrons)	431
		1st Lancers	591
		40th Cacadores	196
ARTILLERY		1st, 2nd, 3rd, 4th and 5th Batteries	807

The majority of French line infantry were equipped with either Charleville IX or XIII pattern muskets. The 12th, 21st and 28th regiments were equipped with 'Voltiguer' muskets as were the cavalry units.

To his left, Beresford positioned a Portuguese division with a British brigade and a small number of cavalry. In the centre, two German battalions of The King's German Legion held the village of Albuera under General Alten. The British 2nd division under General Stewart with its three brigades commanded by Colborne, Houghton and Abercrombie were kept concealed in the rear. To the right, where it was thought an attack was least likely, Beresford positioned the remaining Spanish under the command of Blake along with their own cavalry lead by Loy. General Cole with the 4th Division having arrived rather later than expected, was put in reserve along with all the remaining cavalry units.

At first, the French Marshal Soult tried to trick the British into believing he was making a determined attack on the village centre, but in fact made his main attack under cover of woods and olive groves to Beresford's right, which was held by the Spanish. The French appeared to have some success in making ground towards the village centre and this caused a momentary loss of confidence from the British perspective. Luckily, the French effort at the centre was not sufficient to gain a significant foothold and attention was soon diverted elsewhere.

The French cavalry charged into Loy's Spanish units and the French infantry began to advance in a long column to threaten Blake's right flank. Blake eventually reinforced his right with Zayas's Spanish men, who met this French attack in considerable mayhem, as it was so unexpected. The Spanish very courageously held their ground until the British 2nd Division including the 57th of foot came to their support. These men under General Stewart then attacked the flank of the long French infantry column, which threw it into confusion. Colborne's brigade including the Buffs, began a forward charge, but two French cavalry regiments shielded from sight by a heavy storm came down upon them from the right.

Three British battalions were annihilated in the space of around five minutes as the heavy rain had rendered their muskets useless and they were left in the open without defence against the fierce French cavalry charge. The slaughter continued on an overwhelming scale, so much so that the Polish lancers supporting the French rode down to the rear of Zayas' infantry line and very nearly overran Field

Marshal Beresford and his staff – almost toppling the Queen in this bloody game of chess. Houghton's brigade with the 57th West Middlesex Regiment in the centre began to open fire on the lancers, but some of Zayas' Spanish troops were caught in the cross fire. The British were ordered to stop firing, put in better order and repositioned. The Spanish held firm and maintained their gallant stand, continuing to fight on until eventually ordered to fall back.

At this point there was a brief respite in the battle which allowed the French to recover from the confusion of the first attack. The British used this time to move Houghton's brigade including the 57th alongside and in place of Spanish troops. This was the lull before the storm, as the bloodiest scenes were yet to unfold.

Houghton's brigade with one complete battalion of the 1st Brigade, (in all totalling some 2,000 men) were strung out in a thin red line to hold the ridge against a massed French column of more than four times their number. The Brigadier was mortally wounded early in this action and Colonel Inglis of the 57th took his place. His regiment suffered the worst losses, with some companies losing all their officers as well as two Ensigns, namely Jackson and Veitch who were shot down as they carried the colours. The West Middlesex's regimental colour was pierced by twenty-one musket balls during the battle and the King's Colour was hit by a similar number in addition to having its staff broken. Colonel Inglis acting as

Brigadier had his horse shot from under him but continued commanding the line on foot until he was himself severely wounded. He refused to be carried to the rear for treatment, and remained on the ground where he had fallen in front of the Colours encouraging his men to fight on and shouting his now famous words "take careful aim my boys and die hard 57th, die hard." The 57th including Thomas continued their determined fight regardless of the massive losses and the seemingly impossible task that faced them, simply refusing to give up. Where they fought they fell, with their faces to the foe and their wounds to the front.

"Even as they fought in files they lay,
Like the mowers grass at dawn of day,
When his work is over on the levelled plain,
Such was the fall of the foremost slain."

Lord Byron.

Finally, General Cole was convinced by his staff to bring the 4th Division from reserve and advance them quickly to push the French back. His three battalions of Fusiliers and a Portuguese regiment advanced on the French reserves on the right and by charging down the hill at them in great force, and without warning, drove the French into confusion once again.

At the same time, Abercrombie's brigade moved round to assist in a hammer blow manoeuvre and happily, the resulting chase. The French made a hasty retreat to the olive groves from their main front of attack at the right of the British forces. The earlier French success against the Germans at the village nearer the centre was now of no consequence as they were now in a massive retreat. Victory was imminent and was eventually achieved for Britain and her Allies, but at a terrible cost. Beresford prevented the 57th continuing pursuit of the French into the woodland, shouting *"Stop, stop the 57th, it would be a sin to let them go on"*. Sir William Napier wrote of the battle, *"The rain flowed after in a stream coloured with blood and fifteen hundred unwounded men, the remnant of six thousand unconquerable British soldiers stood triumphant on the fatal hill"*.

The French Marshall Soult had accepted defeat and began his final retreat from La Albuera on the 18th May, leaving the remaining 2,000 unburied bodies of his dead where they lay strewn across the battlefield. He also abandoned over 4,000 wounded Frenchmen unable to serve him further, to whatever fate they could expect to suffer at the hands of the Allies. The British Cavalry followed the French retreat at a safe distance, while most of the remaining British infantry marched north to resume the siege of Badajoz.

Of the 57th Regiment's six hundred and forty-seven men, two officers, namely Major Scott and Captain Fawcett and eighty-seven men were killed. Some twenty-one officers and 318 men were seriously wounded, and of these, Captain Jermyn, Captain Kirby and Lieutenant Sheridan later died of their wounds. In relative terms, this amounts to a huge loss of 66% (two thirds) of the regiment being killed or wounded at the battle, this being made up of 14% killed and 52% badly wounded.

Major General Daniel Hoghton of the 57th was shot from his horse while leading his brigade, but tried to recover and re-mount his steed only to be shot again. He fell back from the stirrups and was carried away for treatment. Having been visibly wounded under both arms, a further ten musket shot wounds were discovered when his tunic was removed. He died among his men of the 57th, 48th and 29th of Foot, on the ridge at Albuera and was buried at the cemetery of San Juan's (St John's) a short distance over the border at Elvas in Portugal, where his final resting place is marked with a stone bearing these words:-

"Underneath is deposited the body of Major General Daniel Hoghton of His Britannic Majesty's service who fell in the Battle of Albuhera on the 16 of May, 1811 at the head of his brigade".

The 57th had won their first battle honour, *"Albuhera, the most honourable of all Peninsula blazons on a regimental flag".* Their distinction on the battlefield earned the regiment the famous nickname "The Die Hards", which has remained with them ever since. Whilst writing his dispatch to Wellington after the battle, Field Marshal Beresford commented,

"Our dead, particularly the 57th regiment, were lying as they fought in ranks; nothing could exceed the conduct and gallantry of Colonel Inglis at the head of his regiment".

General Stewart responded to Beresford's commendation, by way of thanks on behalf of the 2nd Division and particularly the 57th regiment,

"I may safely confess the sense we feel of the honour that you have done to our good endeavour. I am particularly gratified by the single mention you have made of Colonel Inglis and his incomparably gallant regiment".

The day ended with cheers of "God save the King" and many a toast of rum, but the following morning when the smoke of battle had settled, the true magnitude and scale of what had happened was realised. A lone 57th drummer boy is said to have drawn the day's rations for his entire company, which he was able to carry away in his tipped hat – such was the measure of their loss.

Many thousands of the common soldiers killed at Albuera were buried in mass graves at the battlefield, having been stripped of all clothing and left for days lying naked in the open, attracting wild animals and birds. Many corpses and dismembered body parts had to be cremated at the site to prevent the spread of disease. The local Spanish men and women came to the fields from the village to help wash and prepare the British dead for disposal as a mark of respect. They straightened the bodies, closed eyelids and crossed arms, whispering prayers for the dead as they went on. In all some 4,159 British soldiers were killed along with 1,368 Spanish and 389 Portuguese. The French lost more than 8,000.

For his accomplishments at the battle of Albuhera, Field Marshal Beresford was made a Knight of the Bath, one of the highest honours of the British Empire. He was also created a Baron in 1814 and in 1823 he was made a Viscount. William Beresford eventually died on 8th January, 1854 without children and thus his title sadly became extinct.

The world now knew that the French could be beaten in battle and this helped to inspire confidence in the allied Generals. The tide had started to turn and with a continued effort, this could be the beginning of the end for Napoleon. Although Albuera was an amazing victory and a hugely significant event during the Peninsula campaign at the time, Wellington remained focused on the immediate job in hand – namely, the continued efforts to capture the fortress strongholds of Badajoz and Cuidad Rodrigo in order to gain greater control and freedom of movement. Wellington had set out from Fuentes de Onoro on the 5th of May and after several days of reconnaissance and strategic planning through the countryside, he arrived at Badajoz on the 20th, after the Battle of Albuera. General Hill then returned from England on 30th of

May to resume his previous command from Beresford. Reinforced by part of Wellington's main army in the North, the so-called second siege of Badajoz began. Unfortunately, this was no more effective than the previous attempt on the north side at San Christobal and this continued to cause serious British losses as no thought was given to a change in tactics.

The 57th as an element of the 2nd division under General Hill formed part of a covering army, effectively fetching and carrying to service the British siege forces. During this time, the 57th were based at Almedraejo.

The separated but replenished French forces under Soult and Marmount were now expected to join in another concentrated attempt to relieve Badajoz. The threat became so great, that on 19th June, Wellington abandoned the siege and withdrew his entire forces to the old position at Albuera some twelve miles away. The French came close to the British position, but were not confident enough to attack due to their previous experience at Albuera and so began to disperse. The British moved westward across the Guardiana to offer themselves better protection temporarily. The 57th under General Hill were then used to push the remaining French completely out of the province of Extremadura over a period of about eight weeks.

This was eventually achieved with much determination and constant manoeuvre for advantage. As an example, the 57th were at Llerena on 14th July, Fuente del Maestre on 25th July, at Merida on 28th July and again at Fuente del Maestre on 25th August. Wellington moved his main army north again, in an assault on Cuidad Rodrigo in the last days of July. The 57th rested for a time at Villa Viscosa near Elvas in Portugal and received a large draft of fresh men from the 2nd battalion to bring the much reduced 1st battalion back up to full strength. By this time, Lieutenant Colonel McDonald had taken over command of the regiment as Colonel Inglis had returned to England in order to recover from the wounds he sustained at Albuera. When Inglis returned, he was promoted and was charged with the command of an entire brigade.

In 1811, the British army serving overseas had a recorded 21,000 casualties, and this put enormous pressure on recruitment back in England. Many recruits were sourced from Scotland and Ireland, where on the whole domestic conditions were even more desperate than those in England. The level of bounty had to be raised several times to entice new recruits.

It was at this point that the 57th's sister regiment, the 77th of Foot (the East Middlesex Regiment) joined the Peninsula Campaign as part of the British 3rd Division. Their uniform facings were also yellow, similar to those of the 57th, but with the lacings singly spaced rather than in pairs and silver officers' lacings rather than gold. The 77th went on to fight in the major Peninsula actions of El Boden, Badajoz and Cuidad Rodrigo. It is worth noting that the two regiments never entered action together during the Napoleonic period although both were to some extent involved in the various sieges of Badajoz at different times and in differing capacities.

By mid-September 1811, Wellington's army in the north had only managed a blockade of the fortress at Cuidad Rodrigo, once again due to delays in receiving equipment. The French now concentrated their army in an attempt to relieve the fortress city and this forced the British to prepare to retreat. On 25th September, the 77th of foot along with the 5th of foot, the 21st Portuguese infantry regiment, five-hundred cavalry and two batteries of artillery held the main road to Cuidad Rodrigo at a village by the name of El Boden, against a massive attack by 2,500 French cavalry. With great courage and determination they eventually formed two small squares, one British and the other Portuguese, to protect themselves from the cavalry. Remaining in tight square formations they prevented the French cavalry breaking them into small groups which would have become easy prey. Instead, the Allies stood their ground in what must have been utterly terrifying circumstances, and fought a steady retreat back to the main British army over a distance of about seven miles.

Their action had protected the rest of the division from the cavalry attack which provided time for Wellington to move the main army to a stronger position at Alfaiates. This being achieved, the French found themselves at a disadvantage and so withdrew to Cuidad Rodrigo, which was still in French hands. The armies then prepared for winter. The Campaign of 1811 and the British efforts at Bussaco, Torres Vedras, Albuera and El Boden had turned the tide of the Peninsula War and given the French a taste of defeat. This was something they were not previously accustomed to and the resulting shockwave was felt right across Europe. Never again would the French be so bold, and from early 1812 they considered their allied opponents with greater estimation, taking a more cautious approach before committing themselves to action.

Portugal had been liberated and the next two years would now be spent fighting to push the French out of Iberia altogether. The 77th went on to fight during a second attempt on Cuidad Rodrigo in 1812 and succeeded in achieving this first British capture of a significant fortress in the Peninsula. They lost five officers and fourteen men, with some thirty-one men wounded in the action.

Badajoz

Having previously secured Cuidad Rodrigo – one of the two main fortresses necessary to have any chance in an eastward push to force the French to retreat out of Spain, Wellington now wanted the other which had for so long eluded him. Immediately following the capture of Cuidad Rodrigo, Wellington focused the main army's attention once more on Badajoz. The 57th spent most of 1812 keeping check on the remaining French in and around the provincial Extremadura area. They provided service cover for the main army during the last and finally successful siege of Badajoz, but were not involved in the actual fighting or storming of the fortress. The 57th remained in this employment for many months; however the role was an important one as it kept the siege forces supplied and could alert the main army of French movements in the region, thus preventing any relief attempts.

By 16th March, 1812, the main British army had concentrated at Elvas, just over the border in Portugal. The 57th including Thomas formed part of the covering army under Sir Rowland Hill in and around Merida. The third siege of Badajoz was far more successful than those of 1811 as Wellington chose to attack at the Picurina fort rather than the heavily defended fort of San Christobal.

After a few days of little progress due to inclement weather conditions, the British, including the 77th, began their attack on the fortress on 25th March, 1812. A massive artillery bombardment began on the 30th March and by 4th April there were two substantial breaches in the Trinidad and Santa Maria bastions. By the following morning another had been formed between the two. An all out offensive was planned for the next day and so on the 6th April, the whole British force attacked simultaneously from several directions. This completely overwhelmed the French and by the next day the garrison at San Christobal had surrendered. Badajoz had at last been taken.

From the 77th, only three officers and eleven men were wounded. Having entered the war with some 850 men, the 77th could only now muster 183 due to sickness and obvious losses at El Boden, Cuidad Rodrigo and Badajoz. The terrible massacre and ill-treatment suffered by the French and native Spanish during the fall of Badajoz is well documented in history and this remains an unenviable stain on the British record in the region to this day. Whilst visiting Albuera in May, 2004, my brother Paul and I were warned never to speak of the storming of Badajoz in public as it is source of great offence to the locals.

During the siege, in order to provide some kind of relief the French had tried to divert British attention in two directions; Marshall Soult again advancing from the south beyond Albuera and Marmont attacking at Beira in the north. The 57th as part of the covering army under Hill was again posted at Albuera to meet Soult, but once the French had word that Badajoz was now in British hands, they did not commit their forces to an attack. The 77th were sent north from Badajoz to Alfantes along with

Wellington and the main British army to head off Marmont's French forces, but Marmont managed to escape across the Agueda and as far as the British were concerned – out of harms' way. This move northward was the final involvement the 77th had in the Iberian Peninsula campaign. With only around 21% of the regiment remaining, the 77th were sent to Lisbon for garrison duty where it remained for around eighteen months. As the sick and wounded gradually returned along with fresh recruits, the 77th still stood at only 490 strong in October 1813, when it was eventually transported by sea to St Jean de Luz.

During October 1812 the 57th were positioned at Aranjuez a few miles south of Madrid. The British siege of Burgos some 150 miles north of them was going badly and with the French under Marshal Soult now advancing from a point south of Madrid, the British were forced to make a retreat to concentrate their overall forces to form a critical mass capable of holding Soult's army at bay. The 57th travelled westward across the river Guadarama a little way north of Toledo. They then made their way to Salamanca around 120 miles to the northwest.

Luckily they had crossed the river and marched up into the mountains before the much larger French force could reach them. The 57th arrived at Salamanca on 8th November where under General Hill they joined Wellington and the main British army. The weather was particularly poor which made the continued British retreat even more difficult. The whole British force now marched around sixty miles southwest to Cuidad Rodrigo along the most direct route, which is now the E80 dual carriageway. This journey took three days to complete in freezing conditions. Once there, the main army went into winter quarters and the 57th as part of Byng's brigade were sent on another 60 or so miles to Ceclavin, between Zarza la Mayor and Canaveral in the Tagus Valley.

This position seems to be ill-thought out, as in the event of an attack from the north or west, the 57th would have their backs to substantial rivers and lakes, with no obvious chance of retreat or escape. The lakes of Canaveral provide some of the most impressive views I have ever seen with their beautiful calm blue waters set against a back drop of dry rugged rocks and a foreground of fine wind-swept sand. The lakes can be seen in all their splendour from the Madrid to Badajoz railway to the north side of the tracks. When viewing the larger scale map we can see the advantage of the position chosen by the British. From Ceclavin the army can move quickly to advance – to Cuidad Rodrigo, Salamanca or Madrid if the opportunity arose, or if necessary to retreat to Extremadura or Portugal. In either event, they were well positioned to support an advance or concentrate in a defence.

Enough to say that by this time, much of the British army had been forced to retreat almost as far as the Portuguese border, and the great victories of 1811 and 1812 now seemed to count for nothing. The French were returning in massive force. The British and their allies desperately needed more men and supplies to have any chance of keeping a foothold in Spain. Preparations were made for winter and the army braced itself ready for whatever circumstances they might be presented with in the coming spring.

The British Army in the Peninsula War during May 1813

According to records discovered thus far, the British Army in the Peninsula at this time was split into four distinct infantry divisions, each with associated cavalry and artillery units. Wellington remained Commander-in-Chief of all allied forces in the Peninsula with the four army divisions headed by Howard, Hill, O'Callagan and Cole. The Cavalry were commanded by Major-General W. Ponsonby.

The 1st Division commanded by Howard consisted of;

> 1st battalion of the Coldstream Guards,
> 1st Battalion of the 3rd Foot Guards
> 1no. Company from the 5th Battalion of 60th Foot
> 1st, 2nd and 5th battalions of the King's German Legion infantry,
> 1st and 2nd batt'ns of the Kings German Legion light infantry.

The 2nd Division commanded by Lieutenant- General R. Hill consisted of;

- Major Cadogan with:-
  1st battalion of the 50th of Foot,
  1st battalion of the 71st of Foot,
  1st battalion of the 92nd Highland Foot
  1no. Company from the 5th battalion of the 60th of Foot.

- Major-General Byng with:-
  1st battalion of the 3rd of Foot (The Buffs),
  1st battalion of the 57th of Foot
  1st battalion of a Provisional Regiment made up of survivors of the 2nd battalions of both the 31st and 66th of Foot.
  1no. Company from the 5th battalion of the 60th of Foot.

The 3rd Division commanded by O'Callagan consisted of:-

  1st battalion of the 28th of Foot,
  2nd battalion of the 34th of Foot,
  1st battalion of the 39th of Foot
  1no. Company from the 5th battalion of the 60th of Foot.
  6th and 18th Portuguese Foot Regiments
  6th Portuguese Cacadores.

The 4th Division commanded by Lieutenant General Sir G.L.Cole consisted of:-

3rd battalion of the 27th of Foot
1st battalion of 40th of Foot
2nd Provisional Regiment made up of survivors
of the 1st and 2nd battalions of the 53rd of Foot
1st battalion of the 7th Fusiliers,
1st battalion of the 20th of Foot,
1st battalion of 23rd Fusiliers
1no. Company of Brunswick Oels.
11th, 23rd and 7th Portuguese Regiments.

Cavalry commanded by Major-General W. Ponsonby
consisted of:-

- The 5th Dragoon Guards
- 3rd and 4th Dragoon Regiments.
- Von Alten with the 14th Light Dragoons and 1st
  King's German Legion Hussars.
- Major-General Brock with the 1st and 2nd
  King's German Legion Dragoon Regiments
- Major Fane with the 3rd Dragoon Guards and
  1st Royal Dragoon Regiments.
- Brigadier- General D. Urban with the 1st and
  11th Portuguese Dragoon Regiments.

Artillery consisted of the following units:-

- Two batteries of the Royal Horse Artillery,
- One Battery of the Kings German Legion
  Horse Artillery,
- Three batteries of the Royal Foot Artillery

- One battery of the Portuguese Artillery.

Luckily, as we have already alluded, the French advance of late 1812 was halted by the onset of winter and so as usual at that time of year, both armies rested in preparation for the next fighting season and waited for the snow to melt. The British used this time well to replenish their number and gain greater support from the Portuguese to aid the campaign in Spain during 1813. By late May, the combined British and Portuguese forces numbered in excess of 70,000 men, which along with the Spanish began to advance confidently eastward in a trident formation. The 57th, as part of the 2nd Division under General Hill, were included in the left or northern advance and marched through Salamanca and Valladolid then on to Burgos. The French, under the command of Napoleon's brother Joseph Bonaparte, who had been installed as King of Spain, retreated early which allowed the whole British and allied armies to unite and force the French into battle at Vittoria on 21st June, 1813.

The Battle of Vittoria

General Hill commanding the 2nd Division, which included the West Middlesex Regiment, was required to turn the French left, in order to allow the British to make ground and expose a vulnerability in their defensive position. The planned trident formation worked well and after a short stationary period the

French began to fall back due to pressure on their centre and both flanks. The Allies pressed on to take the vacated ground and forced the French to continue their retreat. On reaching the Zadora, the 57th took control of Subijana de Alava and managed to hold the village despite continued French attempts to regain it.

Wellington's force pressed hard at the French centre and left flank against determined enemy resistance and eventually crossed the main road to Bayonne – which they occupied to control all movements in the area. They continued to advance cautiously, gaining more and more control of the firm ground and roads. This reduced the ability of the French to manoeuvre their heavy cannon and stores. In a short time, the only remaining open road offering the French the opportunity of an orderly retreat was blocked and the French were given no option but to flee their positions, leaving all their heavy guns, ammunition and food to the British. The 57th as part of the 2nd brigade followed the French until dusk and camped at Albuzastion.

This was so great a victory that the French could no longer keep a foothold in Spain and could make no further worthwhile stand against Britain and her allies in the Peninsula. Joseph Bonaparte was lucky to escape Vittoria alive, and due to his hurried retreat, he managed to lose both his carriage and a silver chamber-pot in the confusion. The chamber-pot was recovered by the British 10th Hussars and is now on display in a museum in Manchester. The Hussars themselves instituted the tradition of drinking Champagne from a replica of the pot on 21st June every year – as a final insult to the one-time French King of Spain. This continues to this day.

When news of Wellington' success reached the rest of the world, Beethoven wrote his music entitled "Wellington's Victory" to commemorate the battle. This was just a year after Tchaikovsky's famous 1812 overture performance, which itself marked Napoleon's freezing retreat from Russia. A monument was later erected in the main square at Vittoria, where it still stands.

Much of the British army marched with Viscount Wellington to San Sabastian to commence another planned siege. General Hill, with the remaining 2nd Division, moved on to take Pamplona. On 27th June, the 57th were ordered to follow the road which the French had taken in their retreat from Vittoria toward France. The French themselves were now thought to be at Roncesvalles just a few miles from the border.

By 14th July, the 57th had control of a pass leading through the mountains which the French had used to escape. The 57th were then sent forward to hold Val Carlos in a gorge about four miles on the French side, which was roughly eight miles from the expected new French position. They did this with little resistance. Napoleon, enraged by the speed and gravity of the defeat at Vittoria sent Marshall Soult to rebuild and take command of the now fragmented French army. On 25th July, Soult advanced with his reformed army to counter the British move on Roncesvalles, which caused the 57th to fall back from Val Carlos. Light companies were posted under a Major Ackland of the 57th to cover the British retreat, only falling back themselves once the French were along side them and the main army had reached a safe distance. Within two days, the whole of the advanced British force concentrated in a position close to Sauroren near Pamplona.

The Battles of the Pyrenees

Wellington joined General Hill from San Sabastion to clarify what now needed to be done. The British position now in the mountains proved difficult to manage given the military methods of the day and this led to two days of hard fighting in the hills, now known to history as the Battles of the Pyrenees. On 28th July, the French attacked the allied forces at Souroren, driving into a Portuguese brigade and pressing hard on the British infantry ranks.

In response, Wellington sent the 2nd Division including the 57th under Byng along with two regiments from the 4th Division in a rapid charge from higher ground on to the attacking French forces. This pushed the French back sufficiently to end the initial offensive. Both armies were reinforced the following day without resumption in fighting.

On the 30th July, the French tried to change their position in order to relieve the on-going British siege of San Sabastion. The British saw a window of opportunity and General Inglis with a small force attacked two advanced French regiments, pushing them through the nearby valley and back toward the concentrated French position. The 57th as part of Byng's brigade, once again charged from high ground at Souroren and this time with huge French losses, they quickly took control of the village, along with around 1,400 prisoners. The following morning the French made a full retreat with the 57th in close pursuit. The light companies drove the French across the Bidassoa and captured an advanced French line. The West Middlesex stationed themselves at Maya for three days then returned to Roncesvalles, where they remained for three months guarding the pass.

The Battles of the Nive and Nivelle

The French had now crossed the border out of Spain and dug themselves in at Nivelle, to await the allied advance. The British decided to wait until November before commencing an all out invasion of France. On 7th November the 57th left Roncesvalles and by the 10th, after a lengthy march during night time, attacked the French under d'Erlon at Nivelle. The 57th were involved in the assault on the redoubts above Espelette. This was a hard slog with serious losses to the 57th. Major Ackland and Lieutenant Knox along with five men were killed and Colonel MacDonald, two Captains, two Lieutenants and fifty men were wounded. The British were nonetheless successful in their attempt and the French once again retreated, this time to Bayonne.

On the 8th December, the British continued their advance with the 57th crossing the river Nive near Cambo through a deep ford. They marched on to Vieux Moguerre, but part of the division stayed on the other side of the river to guard the crossing and were subjected to a surprise attack by a small number of French on the 10th December. The 57th now held the far right of the British forces and were positioned ready for battle along with two other regiments in a valley between Vieux Moguerre and St Pierre. A large pond had formed in front of them caused by heavy rain making the river Nive rise and burst its banks. The British force under General Hill numbered around 14,000 men at this time, which was less than half the number the French had available by the time the battle commenced.

The fighting was heavy in and around St Pierre and the situation was becoming desperate until Colonel Cameron of the 92nd regiment marched his men down the main road with colours held high and drums and fifes playing. Inspired by this sight, the British pushed forward and drove the French back. Lieutenant Aubin commanding the 57th regiment's light company was picked out for particular commendation by Colonel Cameron at the scene for his assistance in spurring the men on. Cameron's daring courage at a pivotal point in the action raised the British spirit and with this they were able to take a stronger offensive stance. Wellington arrived with reinforcements, and the 57th as part of Byng's brigade were instructed to capture a ridge held by French forces above the flooded area.

Grabbing the Colours of the 31st of Foot, Byng rode gallantly up the hill in front of the 31st, 66th and 57th regiments, and attacked the French flank himself. This began to drive the small French force from its prominent position and he quickly mounted the Colour on the summit of the ridge for Viscount Wellington and General Hill to see clearly. The men cheered him on and followed up. The French now hammered the ridge with artillery shells and grapeshot, but the British held firm and drove the French back even further, with the 57th capturing two French cannon. In all, the British lost around 1,500 men and the French more than 3,000.

The 57th lost seven men and three officers (Lieutenant Sankey and Ensigns Johnson and Pode), with a further officer, Lieutenant Myers later dying of his wounds. Another three officers and one hundred and thirteen men of the 57th were wounded. At Christmas 1813, the 57th were still at Vieux Moguerre having lost over a third of their complement during the 1813 campaign.

In February 1814, the British under General Hill continued their advance into France, and on St Valentines Day they ousted the French from Helette with little resistance. The 57th remained there for a few days to protect the road to St Jean Pied de Port, and were then sent to be issued with new uniforms at St Jean de Luz. Due to the 57th collecting clothing, they were not involved in the Battle of Orthes on 27th February, but did manage to return in time to pursue the fleeing French after the battle and eventually went into action at Aire on 2nd March.

On the 18th March, the 2nd Division was unexpectedly attacked by French forces at Vicen-Bigorre. At about 4pm, reliable intelligence information arrived to the effect that the French were approaching and Captain Liane of the 57th was posted with the light companies to guard the road to Conchez. After a short exchange of fire, and with Lieutenant Aubin who was commanding the 57th light company being badly wounded, the French moved back to a safe distance for the night. The following day another, more serious exchange took place at Tarbes, which resulted in the French under Marshall Soult quickly retreating to Toulouse.

The Battle of Toulouse

With Wellington in command, the British advanced cautiously on French soil, taking time for careful reconnaissance and planning before they reached

Toulouse on 27th March. On the 30th, General Hill's 2nd Division including the 57th regiment were ordered to cross the river Garonne north of Toulouse in order to turn the French left and weaken their defensive position. Difficult ground conditions and topography hindered progress and the attempt was unsuccessful.

Having failed to turn Soult's left, Wellington now decided to launch an attack on the French right using other forces. Meanwhile, the 57th diverted French attention toward themselves by making a feint attack at St Cyprien. This tactic proved to be decisive. The battle of Toulouse was fought on 10th April, 1814 with Britain and her allies finally emerging victorious over the French in France and ending the war. The 57th did not take part directly in the main battle given their involvement in the diversion at St Cyprien, but did cross the river Garonne at one point and forced out the first line of French entrenchments at Toulouse.

A few days prior to this, the French Emperor Napoleon Bonaparte had abdicated due to French retreats on all fronts, and so the war was effectively over before the Battle of Toulouse began. Napoleon was sent into exile on the Mediterranean island of Elba a few days later.

During the earlier British eastern advance, part of the army was needed to undertake the siege of Bayonne and in February, 1814, the 57th's sister regiment the

77th of Foot were sent from St Jean De Luz, (where they had been for three months) to take part. The 77th remained in France until 25th August 1814 and were in fact the last regiment to leave at the end of the Peninsula War. Note that although the term Peninsula War is used, the battles were not limited purely to the Iberian Peninsula. The battles in France following the French expulsion from Spain are recorded in history as the final episode of the Peninsula War, even though they were not actually fought in the Iberian Peninsula.

An estimated 220,000 men lost their lives in the Peninsula Campaign and in all, over two and a half million men were killed during the course of the Napoleonic period in Europe. Sir Arthur Wellesley, The Viscount Wellington, was created "Duke of Wellington" shortly after the battles of Orthes and Toulouse, and Spain bestowed her highest honour upon him – The Order of the Golden Fleece.

After the battle of Toulouse the 57th marched to Bordeaux where they rested for four weeks or so. Some of the men were either given home leave to England or were allowed to have their wives join them in France. In any event, Thomas was able to spend some time with his wife Ann in May or June 1814 as she fell pregnant with their first child Sarah during those summer months prior to Thomas embarking for service with the 57th in Canada. Their daughter Sarah was baptised at St Mary's parish church in Watford High Street nine months later. The parish register shows "Sarah daughter of Thomas Norris – a Soldier, and his wife Ann".

Peninsula War Medals.

At the time, it was not customary for soldiers to be awarded medals for their individual service. However, in the case of the Peninsula War, some officers were decorated. Two differently sized circular gold medals and a gold cross were formally issued at the end of the war. The first medal was given to senior officers and measured about 54mm Ø. It was suspended on a ribbon, with a horizontal bar showing the name of the battle each medal was awarded to commemorate. A separate medal was given for each battle honour bestowed. The second was about 35mm Ø, also with a ribbon and bar, which was given to officers who had served in the field and who had actually commanded a battalion in action. Given the large number of battles that were fought during the Peninsula War, many officers were entitled to several medals and bars. These proved so awkward and clumsy to wear that the authorities instructed that officers were only to wear one medal with a maximum of two bars. If an officer was entitled to three bars, then they were issued with the Peninsula Gold Cross and the circular medal was not to be worn. Those officers entitled to more than three bars were provided with their fourth and subsequent bars separately, which they were allowed to add to the Gold Cross ribbon. In all, 684

Peninsula War Medals were issued; 469 with no bars, 143 with one bar and 72 with two bars. The Peninsula Gold Cross was awarded to 163 officers; 61 without bars, 46 with one bar, 18 with two bars, 17 with three bars, 8 with four bars, 7 with five bars, 3 with six bars, 2 with seven bars and only one person – the Duke Of Wellington was awarded nine bars. In all, there were 12 different battles commemorated by these medals and bars, which included some actions in America and the East Indies. Private soldiers like Thomas would not have received any decoration for their service at this point, although some 34 years later in 1848, the Military General Service Medal (MGS) was issued for army service between 1793 and 1814. Around 25,650 applications were made for this medal at the time and Thomas's would have been among them. The medal shows an image of Queen Victoria placing victory laurels on the Duke of Wellington's head as he kneels before her. The words "To the British Army" are inscribed around this scene with the dates "1793 – 1814" beneath.

British MGS Medal, issued in 1848 for army service between 1793 and 1814. Thomas's medal would have been very similar to this, but with "The Pyrenees" in place of "Salamanca".

The MGS Medal was also issued with commemorative bars or 'clasps' given to all soldiers (of whatever rank) involved in land actions at; Rolcia, Vimeiro, Corunna, Talavera, Busacco, Fuentes de

Onoro, Torres Vedras, Oporto, Albuhera, Cuidad Rodrigo, Badajoz, Salamanca, Vittoria, Pyrenees, Nive, Nivelle, Orthez and Toulouse. Further clasps were added for actions elsewhere in the world including; Chrystler Farm, Chateauguay, Fort Detroit, Egypt, Copenhagen, Sweden and Maida. Thomas Norris would have been entitled to claim the MGS Medal with clasps for Albuhera, Vittoria, Nive, Nivelle, and the Pyrenees, and he would have taken it with him to the Royal Hospital in order to wear it at formal ceremonies, parades and state occasions. He probably bequeathed his medal to the Royal Chelsea Hospital when he died in 1858, but sadly the Napoleonic medals collection was stolen from the hospital during a burglary in the early 1900s. His MGS Medal is probably now in a secret private collection or museum somewhere. Current estimates as to the value of such a medal in good condition at time of writing are in excess of £4,000.00. The Duke of Wellington was awarded fifteen clasps with his medal, which was the highest number issued to any individual. Several of these battle names are skilfully chiselled in to the great columns supporting the Arc de Triumph in Paris. It is a wonderful sight to behold if you have an appreciation of architecture and engineering as I do.

War with the United States

The United States had long supported French interests and their alliance with France had been instrumental in the British loss of the American colonies in the earlier War of Independence. Notwithstanding the achievement of peace in Europe following Napoleon's demise and the decline of French influence on the world stage, Britain was sufficiently concerned about American incursions into Canada, which remained a firmly British territory, that they deployed many thousands of troops to protect the boarder. Several regiments like the 57th travelled to Canada direct from the war in Europe. For these men, another foreign war in such a far-flung corner of the world so soon after a long and treacherous campaign in the peninsula this must have been a very unwelcome posting. Thomas had already served with the regiment for eleven years by this time and along with most of the men at his side, he had probably been hoping to return home to England permanently after the Battle of Toulouse. This was not to be. In late June 1814, Thomas continued his service with the 57th and travelled to Canada where he was stationed for ten months.

As mentioned previously in this book, America had become embroiled in the politics of the British war with Napoleonic France, particularly over the restriction of trade. The American congress passed an embargo act in 1807 in retaliation to counter that issued by the British. This prevented American ships from trading with all European countries including Britain. The embargo proved very damaging to both America and Europe and so the Americans then passed the "non-intercourse Acts" which banned

American trade with Britain and France but relinquished the total trading ban with other European nations.

These policies proved to be useless, as both the British and French maintained their embargos affecting neutral countries – the Americans were too remote to have any real control over this. In 1810, the Americans began to trade with Britain and France again, on the provision that both countries lifted their restrictions against the neutral nations. Britain continued to stop American merchant ships on the premise of searching for Royal Navy deserters, but in fact began to pressgang American seamen into the Royal Navy whilst continuing their blockade of neutral countries.

The American President Madison called for action and asked Congress for a declaration of war against Britain on 1st June, 1812. Some Americans supported him, hoping that a war with Britain could lead to territorial gains in North America, either by battle or by negotiations after a successful war. This caused a political split between the pro-British federalists and the republicans who seemed to favour France. The leading republican at the time, Thomas Jefferson responded:-

"The English being equally tyrannical at sea as Napoleon is on land, and with that tyranny bearing on us in every point of either honour or interest – I say down with England"

With this, the United States declared war on Britain, but were ill-prepared to deal with the consequences of such an endeavour at the time. They had counted on the war in Europe to drain Britain of men and resources for some years to come and had not expected Napoleon's catastrophic failures in the Iberian Peninsula and Russia.

During 1813 the British had concentrated some forces on the American continent, blocking its important east coast trade routes. They were highly successful in the summer of 1814 and after fighting at Blandensburg, they attacked Washington itself and burned the White House. They went on to Baltimore but met stiffer resistance and were forced to give up after the American defence of Fort McHenry. These events inspired Francis Scott Key to write the words to the "Star Spangled Banner" which was eventually proclaimed in law as the official United States national anthem in 1931. Things were beginning to escalate to all out war across the American states by the time Napoleon abdicated. With the war in Europe now over, there was little point in continuing a battle with the Americans over trade embargos with Britain and France. Although Britain had the upper hand, the treasury was struggling to finance the American war as their Peninsula involvement had been so costly. Neither Britain nor America wanted the war now – America could easily lose her independence and Britain could ill afford it. In order to bring about an amicable end to the American war, the treaty of Ghent was signed on Christmas Eve 1814. During the negotiations to draw up the treaty, it came to light that the Americans were not only concerned with the trade issue, but as had been suspected all along, they were plotting a territorial expansion westward and to the north into Canada. Military action ended in mid-February 1815 and the Canadian boarder with the United States has since been observed by both sides. (The British eventually left Canada for good in 1906, but the association with the British Redcoat is still maintained through the red tunics of their famous Mountain Rangers).

Waterloo

Fortunately Thomas' regiment – being stationed in Canada, was not involved in any fighting during this period of war between Britain and the United States and was recalled to Europe once news arrived of Napoleon's escape from Elba and his attempt to regain power in France. The West Middlesex Regiment left Canada sometime in April or May 1815, only arriving in Spithead near Portsmouth, Hampshire in August. By this time Napoleon's rapid return to power in France had united the old Allies and many other countries against him for fear of a second French domination of Europe.

Britain led a combined allied force under the command of the Duke of Wellington to a decisive victory against the French at Waterloo in Belgium on 15th June 1815. Napoleon had made his last stand and the war in Europe was finally at an end. He was sent into exile far from France to the South Pacific Island of St Helena, where he remained until his death on 5th May, 1821 at the age of 51. Nineteen years later his body was returned to France and given a hero's burial in Paris.

Europe enjoyed the so-called 'forty years' peace' following the battle of Waterloo, which remains a giant event in European history. From wars on both sides of the Atlantic, (effectively a first world war) Britain emerged as the single European superpower and this fuelled Britain's own imperial expansion and dominance on a global scale throughout the remainder of the nineteenth century.

Wellington went on to represent Great Britain at the Congress of Vienna in 1814/15 to discuss the peace treaty with France and the other European powers. Returning to his previous career in politics, he became Prime Minister of Great Britain in 1828. He favoured catholic emancipation but opposed parliamentary reform and resigned in 1830. He was Foreign Secretary under Peel from 1834 to 1835, and Minister without Portfolio from 1841 to 1846. He died at Walmer in Kent (coincidentally where my brother Paul lives with his young family) on 14th September, 1852 and he was finally laid to rest with full state honours where his tomb remains today at St Paul's Cathedral in London.

Marshall Soult was exiled after the French defeat at Waterloo but was allowed to return to France in 1819 as he had retained the aristocratic title of Duke of Dalmatia, which had been bestowed upon him by Napoleon in 1807. Soult also became a prominent politician and rose to the office of Prime Minister of France from 1832 to 1834 and again from 1839 to 1847. He was Minister for War from 1830 to 1834 and again from 1840 to1844. He was also Minister for Foreign Affairs from 1839 to 1840. Even during his brief period without high office, Soult was invited to attend the coronation of Queen Victoria in June 1837, which he did almost unimaginably alongside his old adversary, the Duke of Wellington. He was made Marshal-General of all France in 1847, and eventually died on November 26th, 1851, leaving his considerable memoirs.

Return to Watford

As we have said, the 57th did not arrive at Spithead until August 1815 and so fortunately or unfortunately depending on your personal perspective, they were too late to take part in the action at Waterloo. Many of the men would probably have liked the chance to have seen Napoleon in his final defeat after so many years of bitter struggle against him. Without disembarking at Portsmouth, the 57th were transported to Ostend in Belgium, and then marched to Paris, where they joined other

British forces as part of the army of occupation in France. They remained in France stationed at Valenciennes for just over three years and it was during this period that Thomas Norris left the army and returned home to England.

Thomas was invalided out of the army in late 1816, "in consequence of having become worn out in the Peninsula". He was sent to England on 21st October and paid up to the 28th. His formal certified discharge date was 26th November 1816, whereupon, the Colonel of the regiment Sir H.W. Dalrymple (who was disgraced in the first expedition to the Peninsula in 1808) certified that having served with the 57th regiment for 12 years and 345 days, Thomas was no longer fit for further service abroad. On Thursday 19th December 1816, Thomas attended the Royal Hospital in Chelsea, London, for a physical examination to confirm that he was unfit to serve and to register as a Chelsea Out Pensioner in order to claim his army pension. He was granted a pension of 6d (six pence) per day and returned to Watford to resume his life in civvie street. Thomas found work as a general labourer – probably on the farms surrounding Watford and may have gone back to his previous trade of butchery. His son David was born in 1818 and a further daughter, Mary was born in the early part of 1819. Thomas and Ann had started to settle in to family life quite comfortably – after all, they had waited long enough to be together.

Recalled to army service

This homely comfort was short lived and only lasted a couple of years. One day in mid 1819, while collecting his pension from the army post in Watford, Thomas was recalled to army service due to renewed French threats. The Government feared a French invasion of the Channel Islands, but with many British regiments now in far flung corners of the expanded empire, Britain needed to post experienced men to protect her own shores. As they were short of experienced men and given the difficulty and expense of recruitment, they decided to raise veteran battalions made up of old but not incapacitated soldiers to fill the garrisons and help train others. Those who refused to enlist would forfeit their army pensions – which by the standards of the day were quite valuable. In addition, the offer of an enhanced pension was made to those who would willingly rejoin the army. Thomas had no choice and was enlisted in the 7th Royal Veterans Battalion. This time, because he was married and had the responsibility of providing for his young children, his family were able to travel with him to his various postings. The Battalion was sent to Alderney first, then to Guernsey, then on to Jersey where there was a massive build up of troops preparing to resist the anticipated invasion. Thomas was based with the battalion's 8th company at the Greve De Lecq barracks on the north coast of the island.

7th Royal Veterans Uniform

As far as we can tell, the 7th Royal Veterans Battalion uniform consisted of a regency bell-top shako, which had become the standard in August 1815 replacing the "Waterloo" design worn since 1812. Prior to that, it would have been a Stovepipe shako – as per those worn at Albuera. The Regency bell-top design was 8½" tall by 11" across at its highest point. The top was made of black leather with a 2" wide band of yellow around it. The body of the shako was made of beaver skin, with a thin band of yellow at the base. The front had a small lacquered black leather peak. A 12" tall plume of white over red cut feathers was positioned centrally at the front, fastened in place by a black rosette with a silver button bearing the number 7. The shako was also fitted with a chin strap which hung from both sides and fastened under the chin. We are unable to find a detailed account of the shako plate design, but it is likely to have resembled a round of laurels with the number 7 in the centre, surmounted with a crown – probably fashioned in brass.

The tunic (or coatee as they were still called then) was brick red and similar in design to that of the 57th, but with royal blue facings on the collar and cuffs. The lace design was white with a single royal blue line weaved longitudinally through the centre. The lace was sewn into the collar edges and added with square ends to the cuffs and in five rectangular pairs down the front of the coatee. As Thomas was part of a centre battalion company, the coatee shoulders had tufts of pulled wool rather than the more ornate swallows nests or 'wings' normally associated with flank and light infantry companies. As with the 57th uniform, two white belts or cross braces suspended an ammunition box and bayonet baldrick. A rectangular brass belt plate with the regimental insignia (similar to that of the shako plate) was worn at the point these two white belts crossed at the front. As usual, a black stock and gaiters were worn with black boots and grey/blue coloured woollen trousers which buttoned across the front.

During their stay in Jersey, Thomas's young family may have lived outside the barracks area in one of the small villages dotted around the island, as on 4th June 1820, Thomas and Ann's son William (My Great, Great Grandfather) was baptised at Trinity Parish Church. This was the only William Norris recorded on Jersey between 1800 and 1840. I visited the barracks and Trinity Parish Church during a holiday there in October 1993. The barracks remains intact and has an interesting museum with artefacts dating back to the Napoleonic and Regency periods. The Church has been beautifully preserved and it was wonderful to stand on the very spot where my Great, Great Grandfather William was baptised some 185 years ago, with his father Thomas and Mother Ann in attendance.

Eventually, after almost four years, the invasion threat passed and the Royal Veteran Battalions were discharged in 1823. Thomas and Ann then returned to Watford with their children. They set up home in Holts Yard opposite the old vicarage (long since gone) on the east side of the Lower High Street, behind the taverns and shops. Holts Yard was later known as "Court 11" and was once where part of the modern Harlequin shopping centre now stands today. The Harlequin Centre was built in the late 1980s and early 1990s – the construction covered many of the old yard areas including Carey Place, Queens Road, Chaters Yard and Hudson's Yard; all of these were in very close proximity to Thomas's residence in Holts Yard.

To get an idea of where Holts Yard is now, visit the main entrance to the Harlequin centre on the High Street almost opposite Kings Street. Facing the shopping centre, turn left and walk up the High Street about 25 metres or so, crossing what remains of Queens Road. You are now standing where the old entrance to Holts Yard off the High Street used to be. Thomas and Ann remained in Watford for the next 33 years where they raised their family and lived relatively ordinary lives. Their son William married a local girl by the name of Mary Betts who worked on a farm in Cassiobury just north of the High Street. They married at St Marys Parish church in 1844. Thomas's son David never married and had no recorded children either registered or baptised. David is described in later documents as an "imbecile" and may have been either physically or mentally disabled. Thomas's two daughters Sarah and Mary each bore illegitimate sons, Luke and William respectively – both taking Norris as their surname. Sarah remained unmarried but continued living in Holts Yard until her death in the 1870's. Mary eventually married a gentleman by the name of Breakspeare who took on her son William as his own.

The National Census of 1841 shows Thomas and Ann living at Holts Yard with their daughters Sarah and Mary and their eldest son David. Their son William is not shown in the Watford census of the same year, as he was travelling away, working as a rural postal messenger. He was recorded as spending the night at lodgings in Edgeware. The next National Census taken in 1851, shows Thomas and Ann living with Sarah, David and Grandson Luke at Holts Yard. William was recorded at Three Crowns Yard at the bottom of the high street with his own young family, as he had been married almost seven years by this time. William's entry clearly states Jersey as his place of birth. Thomas's daughter Mary and Grandson William had already moved away following Mary's marriage to Mr Breakspeare and so were recorded elsewhere on the census return.

On 22nd March 1856, at the age of 77, Thomas's wife Ann died at Holts Yard. The cause of death was described as palsy, years and infirmity of age. Her daughter-in-law Mary Norris (née Betts), who lived with William at Three Crowns Yard, was present at the death and formally informed the authorities. Both Ann and Mary were illiterate. The death was registered three days later by George Poulton, who noted on the death certificate that Ann was the wife of Thomas Norris, a Chelsea Pensioner and farm labourer. By this time the grave yard at St Mary's parish church had closed (in 1854), and so Ann was buried a few days later in a common plot at the new Fearnley Street Cemetery towards West Watford – now opposite Watford Football Club's Stadium in Vicarage Road. All but Thomas and his daughter Sarah had either flown the nest at Holts Yard or died by this time. Sarah's eyesight and general health were failing through years of close needlework in candle lit rooms as she had worked long hours for many years as a seamstress. Thomas clearly became a burden on the family without his wife to care for him. Soon his own physical and mental condition began to deteriorate and eventually a decision was made for him to apply for In-Pensioner status at the Royal Hospital Chelsea. To be eligible to apply to become a Chelsea In-Pensioner, you must comply with the following requirements and conditions:-

1. You must be male.
2. You must be in receipt of an army service or army service disability pension.
3. You must be over 65 years of age (55years if exceptionally disabled).
4. You must be free from the obligation to support a wife, partner or family.
5. You must have served 12 years full-time in the army over the age of 18.

The Hospital accepted his application as he no longer had either a dependant wife or children and could satisfy all the other requirements. Once a place was available, Thomas was admitted as a Chelsea In-Pensioner on 1st October 1856, just six months after his wife's death. He had just turned 78 years of age.

Royal Hospital Chelsea

The Royal Hospital Chelsea was founded long before Thomas's time in 1682 during the reign of King Charles II, to provide accommodation and care for old soldiers who were no longer fit for service and for those injured in action. When James II came to the throne a few years later, he decreed that a daily allowance should be paid to all soldiers who had served at least 20 years and to those who had become disabled by wounds or unfit for further service. This was the beginning of the army pension for which the Royal Hospital remained entirely responsible until as late as 1955. Prior to all this, the State made no provision for old soldiers and so injured, sick and disabled soldiers generally relied on religious and charitable organisations to provide care for them. Much of this care ended in the sixteenth century due to the dissolution of the monasteries in 1536 during the reign of King Henry VIII. By the time of Queen Elizabeth I, it was accepted that proper arrangements had to be made for old and injured soldiers, which eventually brought about an act of Parliament in 1593 taxing local parishes weekly for the relief of old Soldiers. This tax was not to exceed 6d (six old pence) in the pound which equated to 2.5%, given that there were 240 pence in an old pound.

During the civil war between King Charles I and Parliament, changes to pensions and care arrangements for old soldiers were needed and Parliament agreed that pensions and care should be paid out of national funds rather than local taxes. Further improvements were made following the restoration of Charles II in 1660 with the disbandment of the parliamentary army and the return of previously exiled royalist forces. In the 1660s and early 1670s many of the disabled and elderly soldiers were kept on regimental rolls or directed to garrison duty as a way of continuing to provide them with sufficient money and accommodation. This had the negative effect of reducing the usefulness and performance of the military. The army was already stretched for good resources in terms of numbers of men and levels of fitness. For this reason, King Charles decided to make a determined effort to improve pension and care arrangements in order to allow the army to operate more efficiently. On 22nd December, 1681, he issued a Royal Warrant to authorise the building of the Royal Hospital on a 66 acre site at Chelsea and Sir Christopher Wren (of St Paul's Cathedral fame) was commissioned to design and erect the buildings. Funding the hospital construction proved to be problematic as the King was always in financial trouble. Wren was also an MP and in 1685 he proposed that Hackney Carriages should be licensed and the money raised in doing this should be used to help build and run the hospital.

This was approved and instigated by the government; however, no funds have ever been paid to the hospital from this licensing. In addition the City of Newcastle-Upon-Tyne also undertook to provide 100 wagon loads of coal to the hospital each year in lieu of paying rent to the Crown for the use of the castle there. Further funds were raised by withholding army pay and selling military commissions to wealthy families. From here on, all old, injured, sick and disabled soldiers relying upon an army pension were known as Chelsea Pensioners. By the time the hospital opened in February 1692, there were more army pensioners than the 476 the hospital could accommodate and so Chelsea Pensioners were placed in to two categories; "In-Pensioners" and "Out-Pensioners". In-Pensioners were those admitted to and accommodated at the Royal Hospital having surrendered their right to an army pension. Out Pensioners simply received their army pension and lived in their hometowns as normal. When Out-Pensioners could no longer look after themselves, they could apply to become In-Pensioners once a place was available at the Royal Hospital.

The number of Out-Pensioners increased from 51 in 1703 to 739 in 1708 as the army gradually increased in size to manage the expanding empire. This rose to 14700 in 1763 and by the end of the Napoleonic period in 1816, the total number of Out-Pensioners (including Thomas Norris) stood at 36,757.

Nowadays, the main entrance to the hospital off Chelsea Embankment is a magnificent sight. From the road the main hospital buildings are visible with a memorial dated 1892 situated at the mid point between the road and the buildings. An impressive masonry colonnade forms part of the south-facing elevation with a Latin inscription high above telling the history of the hospital. Further monuments and statues are also in place closer to the buildings with the Union Flag flying high above and flanked by two batteries of cannon (eight in number), four of which were captured at the Battle of Waterloo in 1815.

The Royal Horticultural Society has held its annual Flower Show in the south grounds of the hospital since 1913 and in 1949, the first ever live televised church service was filmed at the Royal Hospital Chapel. Her Majesty Queen Elizabeth II presented the Sovereign's mace to the hospital during her Golden Jubilee year in 2002, and it is now carried at all Royal Hospital ceremonial events. Prior to this, the Royal Hospital held no colours or other regimental device. The hospital also has a museum which was opened in 1866, the entrance to which is dedicated to the memory of The Duke of Wellington and includes six French eagles taken at various battles in the Peninsula and at Waterloo. There are also several

Napoleonic paintings. There is a large collection of around 2,100 medals which have been left to the hospital by former In Pensioners, but all are from post-Napoleonic campaigns, including the Crimean, Maori, Zulu and Boer Wars. Many of the medals are from the two World Wars. The museum is open from 10am to noon and 2pm to 4pm daily except Sundays between October and March and is closed on all Bank Holidays. I must make a note of particular thanks here to John Daniel for his kind assistance during my visit to the RCH earlier this year.

The Final Years

Thomas lived and was cared for at the Royal Hospital Chelsea for just over two years, from 1st October 1856 until his eventual death there on 22nd November 1858. So much had changed during the course of Thomas's life. When he was a child in the 1780's, even the most basic machines were seen as almost space age advances, and yet by the time he died, main line trains had been running for over twenty years. Journeys to haul goods and materials from Birmingham to London, which used to take weeks by road or canal could now be completed in a few hours. What wondrous times he must have witnessed.

In his 81st year Thomas died of chronic bronchitis, with which he suffered terribly for at least fourteen days before he finally expired. How fitting it was that he died in Chelsea, a Sub-district of Middlesex, where his death was formally registered two days later. The head of his death certificate bears the royal coat of arms surrounded by an ornate sword belt with the words Honi Soit Qui Mal Y Pense – which later featured in the Queen's Regiment badge design. The 57th were eventually amalgamated with this regiment as its 4th Battalion in 1966 and have continued to celebrate Thomas's victory on Albuhera Day, the 16th May each year ever since. It is only through this amalgamation that the tradition has survived down the years. With our hero now at last able to rest, thoughts turned to arrangements to bury him with dignity and respect. Prior to 1855 deceased Chelsea In-Pensioners who died at the hospital were buried in the hospital burial plot within the Royal Hospital grounds. However, by 1855 this was already full and arrangements were made for burials to be transferred to Brompton Cemetery.

Thomas's body would have been placed in a simple timber coffin or wrapped in a woollen shroud and transported by hearse from the Royal Hospital main entrance facing the river Thames, westward along the Embankment which was still under construction at the time. The horse-drawn hearse only needed to carry its load a short distance along the route of the Thames before turning north, away from the river and on toward Thomas's final resting place at Brompton.

Brompton Cemetery.

Brompton Cemetery was designed by Benjamin Baud and was established in 1836. The site now includes several listed buildings and monuments of historic interest. It also has a chapel based on the design of St Peter's Basilica in Rome. The cemetery in London SW10 was originally known as "The West of London and Westminster Cemetery" and was one of seven so called "commercial cemeteries" established around the capital to cope with the massive population boom in London during the early to mid nineteenth century. The population in London grew from around a million in 1800 to more than 2.6 million by 1850. Britain's dominance on the world stage meant England prospered and before long, London became the commercial capital of the world. This naturally attracted more and more people to London, and the new found prosperity, international trade and success of industry throughout the empire also encouraged couples to have larger families. Along with this came advances in medicine, the construction of sewers and the provision of fresh water supplies, all of which served to increase life expectancy and reduced the previous high levels of infant mortality. With more people reaching adulthood, so more children were produced with each generation and eventually even more accommodation and cemeteries were needed. London had to expand and the suburbs were formed along with the construction of a new railway network to move people around more easily.

Thomas Norris was buried at a depth of 7' in a common grave on compartment 'F' at the cemetery co-ordinate measurements of 57'6" x 130'0". The cemetery records reference is 19634. The plot where he now lies is known as the "Royal Hospital Plot" and has a large memorial to thousands of the Chelsea In-Pensioners who are buried there. I visited the cemetery on 3rd January, 2005 with my son Alfie and noted the words inscribed on the four elevations of the memorial. They read as follows from the western elevation clockwise to the southern elevation:-

"To the glory of God and in revered and grateful memory of 2625 pensioners of the Royal Hospital Chelsea buried around this spot between 1855 and 1893"

"These veterans having fought for King for Queen for England and for Empire in almost every part of the world came home to die in peace honoured and respected by their fellow countrymen"

"Mysore, Egypt, India, Peninsula, Corunna, Salamanca, Flanders, Waterloo, Nepaul, Burmah, South Africa, Afghanistan, Cabul, Candahar, China, New Zealand, Punjab, Crimea, Alma, Balaklava, Inkerman, Sebastopol, Persia, Indian Mutiny, Delhi, Lucknow"

"Erected by the Chelsea Commissioners on behalf of an adoring nation as a testimony and tribute to valour endurance sufferings & devotion"

The Chelsea Pensioners' memorial at Brompton Cemetery, West London, "erected on behalf of an adoring nation". Thomas Norris is buried just to the left of the memorial beneath the word "Peninsula", within the frame of this picture.

No separate memorial to Thomas currently exists as they were not allowed to be erected at common graves in those days. Formal permission to place a headstone or small memorial at Thomas's precise place of burial has been considered, but having accurately surveyed the ground and set out the recorded grave co-ordinates myself, this is not practicable. Thomas's final resting place at Brompton Cemetery is only a few yards from West Brompton Railway Station and is within ear-shot of the cheering crowds at Chelsea football club's Stamford Bridge Stadium and the Earls Court Exhibition Centre.

The cemetery is open to the public 8am to 8pm in the summer and 8am to 4pm during the winter months. Access can be gained via a gate off Fulham Road on the South side or more conveniently via the main North side entrance off Old Brompton Road – which is only a few yards from the memorial mentioned earlier. To find the memorial from the North gate, walk in the main entrance and take the first path to the right. Follow this as far as it goes to a hedge and turn left at the corner you come to. The path then continues along the length of the Royal Hospital Plot. You only need to follow this about forty yards before you see a small gravel path on the left leading slightly up hill. Step on to the path and look up the hill. The memorial is straight in front of you and you are now standing where Thomas was buried almost 150 years ago. Thomas's grave co-ordinates intersect at a point just half a meter away from the eastern elevation of the memorial (this is a point directly over the centre of Thomas's grave), which was erected in 1893, and he now lies beneath the word "Peninsula" which is inscribed on that monument. A small timber peg painted white now indicates the centre of his grave.

Just nine months after Thomas's death, his daughter-in-law Mary (William's wife) gave birth to a son. They christened him Thomas Norris after his heroic Grandfather on 20th August 1859 at St Mary's Parish Church in Watford. And so his name lived on.

The Next Generations

6. The Next Generations

As discussed in chapter 5, Thomas's daughters Sarah (1815) and Mary (1819) each had illegitimate sons, Thomas's son David (1818) remained single throughout his life and had no recorded children.

William Norris (1820 – 1884)

The only legitimate grandchildren to spring from Thomas's direct line were those born to his son William – my Great, Great Grandfather. The National Censuses of 1851, 1861 and 1871 show William and his wife Mary living at Three Crowns Yard, with the family expanding as time went on. William himself was born in Jersey in 1820 and grew up in Watford from the age of about three. In time he somehow managed to gain a basic education – probably through charitable means and learned how to read and write. In 1839 at the age of 19, he started work with the post office as a Rural Postal Messenger. Earning 12 shillings per week, his job involved delivering post to outlying villages and farms within about a ten mile radius of Watford. On 9th November 1844, William married Mary Betts at St Mary's Parish Church in Watford. They set up home in Three Crowns Yard off the lower High Street and remained there for many years before moving to Holts Yard in the mid to late1870's. Their marriage produced seven surviving children:-

Ellen (1847)	Susan (1852)
William (1854)	David (1857)
Thomas (1859)	Luke (1862)
*George (1864)	

William and Mary had two other sons prior to 1859, both named Thomas who did not survive infancy and so it was clearly important to them for the name "Thomas" to be passed on through the generations of our family. William remained with the post office for 35 years and eventually retired due to ill health in March 1875. William's daughters Ellen and Susan are described as Silk Throwsters who, from the age of nine, worked at the silk mill at the bottom of Watford High Street. The children had to stand on tall stools and benches to be able to reach the machinery they had to work. The normal working day was twelve hours long starting at 6am sharp. If you were late you would not be allowed to work that day and so would lose a days' pay – you would also be fined a further days' pay for not attending work. Only Sundays were set aside for rest each week.

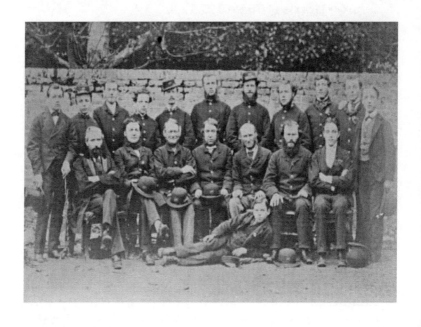

Photograph of Queen's Road Post Office staff c1870. William Norris is pictured at bottom row centre aged 50 years. He had already served 31 years with the Post Office by this time and eventually retired five years later.

William died on 31st January 1884, at the old family residence in Holts Yard, where his mother Ann had died some 28 years earlier. He was just 64. The cause of death is recorded as acute bronchitis, the same complaint that claimed his father's life in 1858. William was buried on 2nd February 1884, in common ground at the Vicarage Road/Fearnley Street Cemetery in Plot No. 113D.

George Norris (1864 – 1929)

George Norris, my Great Grandfather, was born on 2nd May 1864 at Three Crowns Yard off Watford High Street. He was the last of the children born to William and Mary. George was raised in Watford with six siblings and attended the local Dissenters Ragged primary school in Farthing Lane. At the age of eleven, he was employed as a builder's labourer and eventually became a bricklayer. George enlisted in the army, joining the 66th of foot, The Berkshire Regiment in 1882 at the age of 17. He served in the Egypt and Sudan campaigns of 1882, which were directed by General Kitchener, and was decorated with the Sudan Campaign Medal and the Khedives Star. We have found records of his misconduct at Gibraltar, where he was imprisoned for two weeks due to his involvement in a bar brawl. George left the army in 1890 and went back to the building trade. At the age of 27, George married Elizabeth Smith on 2nd January 1892 at the Primitive Methodist Chapel in Queens Road, Watford. Elizabeth was 18 years of age. She already had an illegitimate daughter – reputedly by George's brother Thomas and It would appear that for some reason, George had offered to take on his brother's responsibility – possibly out of duty if his brother had abandoned her, or perhaps even died before marrying her himself. They lived at No.5 Court 15 (previously known as Boot Yard) off the east side of the High Street between Three Crowns Yard and Holts Yard. Their marriage produced some seventeen children over a twenty-one year period, although only seven of them managed to survive their early years. This equates to around twelve years of constant pregnancy. The Children were named as follows:-

Daisy May (1890) – Illegitimate

Mary Elizabeth (1892),	Susan Rose (1893)
George (1894)	William (1895)
Frederick (1896)	Arthur (1898)
Gertrude (1899)	Albert (1901)
Dorothy Ruth (1902)	*Sydney Herbert (1903)
Bertha (1905)	Lesley (1907)
Percy (1908)	Francis (1910)
Gladys Ada (1911)	Ernest Charles (1913)

Only Daisy May, William, Frederick, Gertrude, Sydney, Bertha and Francis survived infancy. The family had moved to No. 52 Shaftesbury Road by 1903 when Sydney was born and by 1907 they had moved to No.22 Fearnley Street.

Upon the outbreak of war in 1914, George re-enlisted in the army, joining the Hertfordshire Territorial Regiment on the 9th November at the age of 50. Having served as best he could in recruitment and training, he was discharged three and a half years later, on 15th June 1918 due to ill health. George's eldest sons William and Frederick also joined the army in the early part of the First World War – probably at their father's request. William was caught in artillery fire during his service in France and was buried alive in the trenches – only to be dug out two days later by British troops. He had lost his right hand and several fingers from his left. He also had to have special steel plates inserted in his head to repair his skull where he was hit by shrapnel, but still somehow managed to survive. The Book of Abbots Langley includes a picture of him in the 1920's as Grand Master of the Royal Antediluvian Order of Buffaloes. William's brother Frederick was sadly killed in action in France on 30th June 1918 aged 22 years. Private Frederick Norris 4/6917, of the 2nd Bedfordshire Regiment (6th & 9th platoon) was posthumously decorated with the 1914/15 Star, which was sent to his mother with a formal note of thanks for "services rendered" in defence of his King and Country. Fred was buried in Plot 4, Row H, Grave 8 at Warloy Baillon Cemetery, which is located approximately 13 miles from Amiens and 6 miles from Albert in the region of the Somme.

At the end of the war, George returned to the building trade. He became quite portly in his later years and is known to have been a heavy drinker. As a boy, my Grandfather Sydney often had to sit outside the public houses on Watford High Street late into the night, waiting for his father to finish his drinking sessions. Sydney would then lead his father home by the hand, to make sure he got home safely – such was his level of intoxication. George tended to be somewhat autocratic in his behaviour and this along with his excessive weight and ill-health did little to help his relationship with his wife Elizabeth.

The couple split in the early 1920's and again due to ill-health, George became unemployed. He received financial assistance through the newly amended National Insurance Act. George died aged 64 years, on 4th March 1929 at No. 22 Fearnley Street in Watford. His cause of death was Broncho Pneumonia and Chronic Bronchitis – the third successive generation of this direct line to die of the complaint. George was buried in Plot No. 758D with his brother Thomas at the Vicarage Road Cemetery a few days later. Note that George died of the same illness at the same age as his father.

George Norris (c1889) aged about 25 years, wearing his Berkshire Regiment uniform along with Sudan Campaign and Khedives Star medals. Note the Berkshire Regiment (The 66th of Foot) were also present at the Battle of Albuera some 70 years earlier.

Private Frederick Norris 1896 - 1918

161

George's son Fred was killed in action during WW1. His grave at Warloy Baillon cemetery in the region of the Somme is well tended by French locals, as are many thousands of others, which mark the final resting places of so many of our nation's brave heroes.

Sydney Herbert Norris (1903 – 1975)

My Grandfather Sydney Herbert Norris was born at No.52 Shaftesbury Road, Watford, on 8th December 1903. He was the fourth surviving child of George and Elizabeth and attended Watford Fields School (later known as Victoria) School along with his younger sister Bertha until the age of 14. Sydney was a very bright young man, but made little use of his academic gifts as he chose to pursue a career in catering. He moved to Holborn in London to work as a Chef at a hotel at No.2 Myddleton Square, not far from Kings Cross. It is believed that Sydney was additionally employed in this capacity by a nobleman (possibly an Earl) who also had a house in Holborn. He worked there with a young lady by the name of Lily Tighe who was about six years younger than him, and who had come from Chesterfield in search of employment. Before long, a romance had sprung and they were married on 19th January 1929 at St Mark's Parish Church, also in Myddleton Square. Their marriage produced five children, these being my Uncles Reginald (Ginger), Anthony (Snowy) and Brian (Prof) along with my Aunt Rosemary and of course my own Father. After the birth of Reginald, Sydney returned to Watford with Lily and the baby, living first at No.103 Gladstone Road, then moving to No.2 Gorle Close in about 1935. He worked briefly as a window cleaner in Watford, before the outbreak of the Second World War.

When war was declared in 1939, Sydney was drafted in to the Auxiliary Fire Service (AFS) and spent a good deal of time fighting fires in London during the Blitz. An AFS base was set up in a commandeered garage on the North Orbital Road in North Watford, opposite the Kingswood housing estate, and this is where Sydney's operations were managed from. The garage building remains intact and is situated next to the Esso petrol station off Sheepcot Lane at Leavesden in North Watford. On one particular fire call during the blitz in London, Sydney was in command of fire fighting forces trying to extinguish a fire at a multi-storey building which was raging out of control. Several people were trapped in the basement of the building with no hope of escape and it was too risky to send firemen in to rescue them as the building was about to collapse. Sydney was forced to give the order for the water hoses to flood the basement and drown the poor souls who were trapped there – thus saving them the agony of being slowly roasted alive. He never forgave himself. On a separate occasion, Sydney rescued a middle aged lady from another burning building, receiving multiple burns himself. Then, once outside, he tended to the lady's injuries. She had horribly burned hands and legs and her hair had caught fire. As he began to bandage her wounds, they could both hear a bomb whistle as it dropped from an enemy aircraft overhead. The usual procedure at that point would be to cover ones ears with your hands and lie down on the floor – quickly bracing yourself for a large explosion at close quarters. The injured lady was unable to cover her ears due to her terrible burns, so Sydney covered them tightly with his hands and thus, as the bomb hit the ground he allowed his own ears to be blown out by the blast in order to save hers. From that moment on my Grandfather was completely deaf – but was always adamant that he had done the right thing on that day. Sydney was seconded to work with the De Havilland aviation company, who were engaged in the production of military aircraft at Leavesden. In time he was promoted to the post of Chief Fire Officer, responsible for the Dehavilland (later Rolls Royce) aerodrome at Leavesden and others at Aldenham and Hatfield. The famous Dam Buster's "bouncing bomb" was developed and tested at Leavesden during Sydney's time there. At the end of the war, he returned to his previous occupation as a window cleaner. Sydney maintained his special relationship with his sister Bertha throughout their lives and when I visited my Great Aunty Bertha as a child with my parents in the 1970's, she would often recall the mischief they used to get up to together all those years ago.

In 1964, Sydney and Lily divorced after some 35 years of marriage. He married his second wife Sibyl in the late 1960's and lived out the remainder of his life at Gorle Close, where he retired and enjoyed his keen interest in gardening. He was a superb cook, a good, hard working man and by all accounts a teetotaller. At the age of 72, Sydney died of a sudden heart attack on 7th May 1975 at Gorle Close where he had lived for around 40 years. He was cremated in Watford.

Sydney Herbert Norris, my Grandfather. Photograph taken c1941, in Auxiliary Fire Service (AFS) uniform.

The Thomas/Moses Enigma

7. The Thomas/Moses Enigma

Throughout much of this study I have been dogged by the nagging thought that some readers might doubt or perhaps even challenge the link between Thomas and Moses, given the complexity of this story. In truth, for some time I had my own concerns in this respect and so, along with my Uncle Brian I set about a more detailed investigation to prove (or disprove) the theory that Thomas and Moses were one and the same person. We believe that Thomas Norris used the name Moses when he joined the army in 1803 and continued to use it as an alias in all his military dealings until he died in 1858. Our aim was to prove this theory "beyond any reasonable doubt" – which was the best we could possibly have hoped for as it would be as difficult as conducting a court case with both a prosecution and a defence, each testing the other to get to the truth of the matter. I have taken the opportunity here to explain the course of the research we carried out and the relevance of the information discovered. In addition to this, I have included some copies of the old documents we found along the way with an indication of their source and any useful documental cross referencing. Generally, our investigation is founded on information contained in parish and military records, as well as civil registration documents and census returns. These initially connect both Thomas and Moses with the following circumstances:-

- Both lived in the same town and were about the same age.
- Both had wives and children with the same names and ages.
- Both were referred to as Soldiers & Chelsea Pensioners.
- Each had a son named William born on Jersey in 1820.
- Both are recorded as being employed as Butchers.
- There are only baptism and marriage records for Thomas.
- There is only a death record for Moses.

Even without a detailed explanation, the evidence is quite compelling given the numerous ways these two characters are connected. It is necessary however to give a full account of how we arrived at our conclusions in order that you can better understand the theory and know for certain that no other explanation is possible. To start with, we went back to basic principles. We searched for a marriage certificate for my Great, Great Grandfather, William Norris and his wife Mary Betts in Watford prior to 1864, which was the year my Great Grandfather George was born. George's birth certificate shows William and Mary (nee Betts) as his parents. We found their marriage registered in Watford in 1844. The certificate shows William's father as our "Thomas Norris". The next stage was to find a record of birth or baptism for William. Normally, the way to do this would be to check how old William was at the time of his marriage in 1844, this information is usually given on marriage certificates.

Unfortunately, the marriage certificate does not give his precise age, it simply states his age as "full". This means he was twenty-one years of age or older. Because we knew William was married and lived in Watford, we checked the 1851 national census return for Watford and found a record showing William and his wife Mary living at Three Crowns Yard in the Western back-drop to the lower high street, behind the Three Crowns public house. William is shown as head of his household aged 31, living with his wife Mary, daughter Ellen and Brother-In-Law David. This means that William was born in or about the year 1820 {1851 (year of census), less 31 (William's stated age) =1820}.

The census return also notes that William was born in Jersey. As a check, we looked for a baptism record for a William Norris in Watford between 1800 and 1840, but no such record exists. Next, using our contacts with the Channel Islands genealogical societies we found the only record of a William Norris ever being baptised on Jersey was in fact in June 1820 at Trinity Parish Church. This William is recorded as the son of Moses Norris, a private soldier of the 7th Royal Veterans Battalion and his wife Ann. With this information, we traced Moses' army career and personal details using muster rolls and pay lists. This is where we learned about his Peninsula service with the 57th during the Napoleonic War and that on pain of losing his army pension, after he was invalided out of service with the 57th in 1816, he had been recalled to serve in the 7th Royal Veterans Battalion in 1819. We then looked at Moses' 1816 discharge papers and Chelsea Royal Hospital pension records, taking note of every tiny detail. We can see immediately that all available military service and pension records refer to a Moses Norris who was born in Watford. It is also plainly apparent that there are no military or pension records anywhere for a Thomas Norris throughout his known lifetime – and yet in 1815, Thomas and Ann's daughter Sarah was baptised in Watford as the child of "Thomas Norris, a Soldier". Thomas using the name "Moses" would have been serving in Canada at the time of the baptism and his wife Ann would have had to explain why her husband was not in attendance at the service. Note that Sarah would have been conceived in the same month that "Moses" rested from army service between leaving the Peninsula and embarking for Canada.

Now we needed to look at Thomas's own marriage records. As one would expect, no marriage certificate exists for this event as it took place before the advent of civil registration. However we found an old parish register showing Thomas Norris, a "Butcher" from Watford marrying Ann Buck, at St Mary the Virgin Parish in Henley-on-Thames in 1802. We checked back to the 1841 and 1851 census returns and found that Thomas's wife Ann, who lived with him at Holts Yard in Watford was noted as "born in Henley". This confirms that the Thomas Norris and Ann who married in Henley-On-Thames were the same Thomas and Ann Norris who lived at Holts Yard in Watford and who had a son named William (my Great Great Grandfather) who was born in Jersey in 1820.

All of Moses' military and pension papers (from 1803 to 1856) show his profession prior to joining the army as being a Butcher. This was the same trade Thomas claimed to have in 1802 when he married Ann Buck in Henley–On-Thames. Moses Norris continued to claim his army pension in his hometown of Watford until late 1856, when he became a Chelsea In-Pensioner and went to live at the Royal Hospital, where he eventually died in 1858. No records of any census returns exist for Watford or anywhere else to show a Moses Norris ever existed at that time. Moses was only ever recorded in Military and army pension documents, with the exception of the rogue baptism of William in Jersey – who we have established was without doubt the son of Thomas and Ann, even though the register gives Moses Norris as the father. In 1856, when Ann Norris died in Watford, her husband Thomas vanishes from the pages of history. The last documented use of his name was on Ann's death certificate – which reads "Ann, wife of Thomas Norris a Chelsea Pensioner". There are no death or burial records for Thomas

Norris before or beyond this point, but he must have eventually died of something and he must have been buried somewhere.

Remarkably, a few months after Ann's death, Moses Norris of the same age was admitted as an In-Pensioner at the Royal Hospital Chelsea "no longer having a dependant wife or children". We believe this is conclusive proof that both men cannot have existed simultaneously between 1803 and 1858 as records can only account for one of them at any given time. The similarities in their lives are well beyond the realms of coincidence as they extend to locations, relationships and life phases, all of which mesh together to show that Thomas and Moses were the same man. For ease of reference I have included a table of information below to chart the recorded events in chronological order. As you will see the puzzle falls into place very easily. Where Thomas is recorded, Moses is not and where Moses is recorded, Thomas is not.

Year	THOMAS Events/Records	MOSES Events/Records
1776		Baptised in Watford
1778	Baptised in Watford	
1799		**Buried at St Mary's Watford**
1801	Thomas arrested	No records
1802	Thomas marries Ann in Henley- On-Thames	No marriage record ever found.
1803	No records	Moses Joins 57th Regiment
1804	No records	Moses on muster rolls and pay lists with 57th.

1804 – 1814	No records for Thomas. No children recorded	Moses fully documented in army with 57th. States born in Watford.
1814	No records for Thomas.	Moses has short rest from service before embarking for Canada.
1815	Thomas shown as soldier on daughter Sarah's baptism.	Moses serving in Canada
1816	No records	Moses returns from Canada and is invalided out of the army.
1816	No records	Moses – Chelsea Out-Pensioner.
1818	Thomas's son David baptised in Watford.	No records
1819	No records	Moses recalled to serve with the 7th Royal Veterans Battalion in Jersey.
1820	No records	William baptised in Jersey the son of Moses Norris a private soldier.
1841	Thomas and Ann on census return	No Census records
1842/51	No records	Moses pension paid in Watford.
1851	Thomas and Ann on census return for Watford. Shows son William born in Jersey in 1820.	No Census records
1856	Ann wife of Thomas Norris a Chelsea Pensioner dies	No records
1856	No further records are ever made referring to Thomas	Moses Norris admitted as Chelsea In-Pensioner.

1858	No records exist for Thomas's death or burial anywhere	Moses Norris dies at Chelsea Hospital.

I have included details in these next few pages from the various important military documents discovered. Unfortunately, due to the deterioration of these documents over time and the quality of third generation copying, we are unable to reproduce the documents clearly in this book as I would have preferred. Copies remain on file should they be required for any future research. By kind permission of the National Archive, these are scanned photocopies of the microfilm images taken from the originals held at the PRO at Kew.

Muster Rolls and Pay Lists 1804. (overleaf)
1st Battalion of the 57th Regiment of foot covering the period from 25th January to 24th February 1804. This shows Thomas Norris (alias Moses Norris) was paid one shilling per day from 5th to 24th February, which amounts to £1 as there were twenty shillings in one old English pound. The War Office reference for this document is W012 – 6640, which is held at The Public Record Office in Kew.

No.	Rank and Names.				£.	s.	d.					Remarks
	Brought forward				57	9	2	31		528		
15				31	1	11				31		
16				11		11				11		
17				31	1	11				31		
18				31	1	11				31		
19				31	1	11				31		
20				20	1					20		
21				20	1					20		
22				20	1					20		
23				15		15				15		
24				31	1	11				31		
25				31	1	11				31		
26				31	1	11				31		
27				31	1	11				31		
28				20	1					20		
29				11		11				11		
30				31	1	11				31		
31				11		11				11		
32				31	1	11				31		
33				31	1	11				31		
34				11		11						
35				20	1							
36				11	1							
37				31	1	11						
38				11		11						
39				20	1							
40				1		1				1		
41				11		11				11		
42				31	1	11				31		
43				31	1	11				31		
44				11		11				11		
45				10	1	10				10		
46				31	1	11	31			31		
47				11		11				11		
48				31	1	11				31		
49				31	1	11				31		
50				15		15				15		
51				20	1					20		
52				20	1					20		
53				20	1					20		
54				1		1				1		
55				1		1						
56				20						20		
57				31	1	11				31		
58				31	1	11				31		
59				31	1	11				31		
	Carried forward	£	86	6	2	62				600		

176

Muster Rolls and Pay Lists 1816.

57th Regiment of foot, Muster Rolls and Pay Lists for the 1st Battalion, covering 25thSeptember to 24th December 1816. Recorded at Valenciennes, France. War Office reference is WO12 – 6646. This document is held at the Public Records Office, Kew. Private Moses Norris is shown as being paid from 25th September to 28th October 1816. He is recorded as absent from the last three musters due to "command" – meaning he was either obeying orders in service separately from the remainder of the battalion or was possibly in sick bay and unfit for muster. It is also noted that he was sent to England on 21st October and paid until 28th October 1816. The document gives his rate of pay as 7d (seven pence)

177

per day and this has been multiplied by 34 days to give 19s 10d (nineteen shillings and ten pence). Note that the Old English pound sterling was made up of twenty shillings and each shilling was made up of twelve old pence. In this case, 34 days x 7d = 238 old pence, which was just 2d short of a whole pound. This document records all men recruited who should remain in service including one of Thomas's comrades – William Neal, who was listed as being a prisoner of war for four years since 17th November, 1812. Others like Private James Murray are shown as sent to England for recovery since 20th August, 1811. Both these men were not allocated payments in the register and clearly if soldiers were sick or captured by the enemy, their army pay was withheld – all the more reason not to get caught or go sick! In comparison with the pay lists of 1804, Thomas was being paid 5d less per day in 1816 directly before he was invalided out of service.

Royal Hospital Chelsea soldiers documents 1760 – 1913.

War Office reference WO97, piece 702, held at the Public Records Office, Kew. The document reads. "I Moses Norris do acknowledge that I have received all my clothing, pay, arrears of pay and all just demands who-so-ever, from the time of my enlisting in the regiment mentioned on the other side, to this day of my discharge. As witness my hand this twentieth day of October 1816, Moses (his X mark) Norris." There are two illegible witness signatures. The document continues…"I do hereby certify that the cause which has rendered it necessary to discharge the within mentioned Moses Norris as stated on the opposite side, has not arisen from vice or misconduct and that he is not to my knowledge incapacitated by the sentence of a court martial from receiving his pension." This is signed illegibly by the surgeon and commanding officer. Note: this was held on file at the Royal Hospital Chelsea from 1816 to 1856, following which the words below were added in a different hand-writing:- "Admitted as In-Pensioner 1st October, 1856". The lower portion of the document has handwritten information at right angles to the main body of text, which also appears to be part of the original 1816 entry. The words read… "57th Foot, Moses Norris aged 44, Service 13. Weekly pay ended on service in the Peninsula, 6d. Watford, Hertfordshire, Butcher." Note the age was estimated by the surgeon based on Thomas's physical appearance.

Statement of Service 1816.

War Office reference WO97 – 702. The document reads: "His Majesty's 57th Regiment of foot, whereof Sir H. Dalrymple is Colonel. These are to certify that Moses Norris, private in Major James' company in the regiment aforesaid, born in the parish of Watford, in the county of Hertfordshire, hath served in the said regiment for the space of 12 years and 345 days as likewise in other corps according to the following statement, but in consequence of having become worn out in service in the Peninsula, is considered unfit for further service abroad". Note the only Moses Norris ever recorded as born in Watford was Thomas's brother who died in 1799. The document goes on to describe his estimated age, height, eye colour, hair colour and complexion as previously stated in other documents. His full service with the 57th is recorded as being from 16th December 1803, until 20th November 1816, with a formal certified discharge on 26th November 1816.

Royal Hospital Chelsea Regimental Registers 1715 to 1857.

War Office reference 120, piece 26 held at the Public Record Office, Kew. The document is dated 19th December 1816 for the 57th Regiment of foot. Moses Norris is shown at estimated age of 44 years (actually 38 years) with thirteen years service. He was granted a pension of 6d per day. Further details show he was previously a Butcher from Watford, and was now no longer fit for army service.

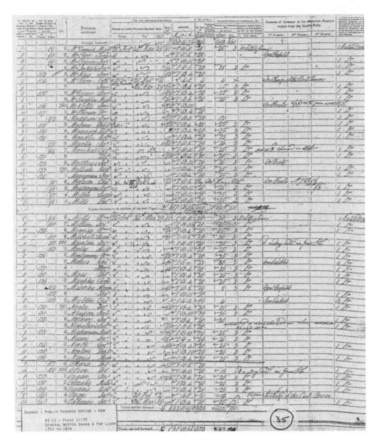

Admissions Book for Royal Hospital Chelsea 1816.
War Office reference WO 116 –24, held at the Public
Records Office, Kew. The page is entitled
"Examination of Invalid Soldiers on Thursday 19th
December 1816" Again Moses is shown at an
estimated age of 44 years with 13 years army service
– predominantly in the peninsula. He is described as
five feet eight and a half inches tall, with grey eyes,

Brown hair and a dark complexion. Once more, his previous employment is given as a Butcher from Watford, Herts. Here too, he is shown as being entitled to a pension of 6d per day.

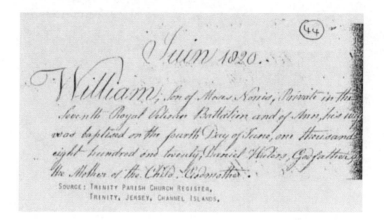

SOURCE: TRINITY PARISH CHURCH REGISTER,
TRINITY, JERSEY, CHANNEL ISLANDS.

Baptism Register, Trinity Parish Church, Jersey 1820.

Provided by the Channel Islands Family History Society. It is the only record of a William Norris baptised on Jersey between 1800 and 1840. The entry reads, "Juin 1820. William son of Moses Norris Private in the Seventh Royal Veterans Battalion and Ann his wife, was baptised on the fourth day of June One Thousand Eight-hundred and twenty, Daniel Waters Godfather and the Mother of the child Godmother."

185

Royal Hospital Chelsea Out Pensioners Register.

This volume contains records from 1842 to 1852 for army Out Pensioners in the London area. War Office ref WO22 – 56, held at the Public Records Office, Kew. The document shows Private Moses Norris previously of the 57th of foot being paid his pension at the rate of 6d per day. His date of admission as an Out-Pensioner is shown as 19th December 1816. This page indicates that Moses Norris was included in the 1st North London army pensioner's district and specifically shows this district as Watford, Hertfordshire. According to the register he was paid up to the 30th June.

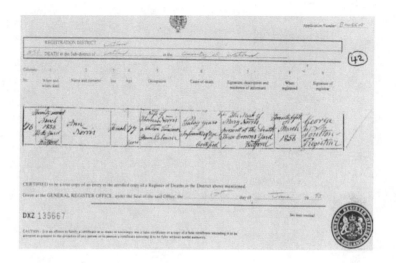

Death Certificate for Ann Norris dated 25th March 1856.

Obtained from the Public Records Office, St Catherine's House, Holborn. Ann is recorded as having died on 22nd March 1856 at Holts Yard, Watford at the age of 77 years. Cause of death is shown as being due to "Palsy, years and infirmity of age". Interestingly, Thomas and Ann's daughter-in-law Mary (wife of their son William) registered the death and is noted as having been present at Holts Yard when Ann died. Ann's occupation is recorded as "wife of <u>Thomas</u> Norris, a Chelsea Pensioner and farm labourer". No records exist at Chelsea Hospital for a Thomas Norris, only a Moses Norris.

Royal Hospital Chelsea Pensioners Register 1780 – 1876.
War Office Reference WO23-146 held at the Public Records Office, Kew. This document shows Moses Norris of the 57th of Foot as entitled to a pension of 6d. per day. This records Moses as having been admitted as an Out-Pensioner on 19th December, 1816, then some forty years later becoming an In Pensioner on 1st October, 1856. His pension reference number is given as F31566. The document goes on to state that Moses remained as an In

Pensioner residing at the Royal Hospital Chelsea until 22nd November, 1858 where he eventually died.

Death Certificate for Moses Norris dated 24th November 1858.

Obtained from the Public Records Office, St Catherine's House, Holborn. The document shows that Moses Norris died 22nd November 1858 at the Royal Hospital Chelsea. Cause of death was Chronic Bronchitis, which would in years to come, also claim the lives of his son William in 1884 and his grandson George in 1929. This certificate contains a simple clerical error in the surname field. The name 'Morris' is written instead of 'Norris'. This need not distract our lines of research as no other records exist for a Moses Morris at our three information sources, namely – Civil Registration documents, Military Records and Royal Hospital Chelsea registers. (It is highly unlikely that both a Moses Norris and a Moses

Morris both died at the same hospital on the same day, at the same age with only one death certificate issued). The Royal Chelsea Hospital confirms this is a spelling error. Thomas Norris (AKA Moses Norris) was buried at Brompton Cemetery, Old Brompton Road, London SW10 on 26th November, 1858.

A Brief History of The Middlesex Regiment

8. A Brief History of The Middlesex Regiment

The original 57th infantry regiment was raised during the eight year long War of Austrian Succession but was renumbered the 46th at the end of the war in 1748, when the total number of British infantry regiments was reduced to fifty-one. This effectively ended the brief existence of the original 57th regiment. Just seven years later, in 1755, war with France caused the number of regiments to be increased again, this time to sixty-one and thus another new 57th regiment was formed. In 1757, the 50th and 51st British infantry regiments were disbanded, which caused the other regiments (52nd to 61st) to be renumbered. In particular, the 57th became the 55th and the 59th became the 57th. This is where the story of the West Middlesex Regiment begins – at the formation of the 59th of Foot just prior to this renumbering exercise in 1756.

The 59th of Foot was created at the very end of 1755 with the appointment of Colonel John Arabin to the new regiment sometime in December. In early 1756, officers were appointed and two companies of men were provided to begin recruitment and training. The first company was brought in from the 3rd of Foot (the Buffs) and the second company were from the 20th of Foot (the East Devonshires). The 59th regimental uniform facings were 'lemon' yellow as was the original 20th of Foot uniform and in time this featured in the collars, cuffs, lapels, swallows nests (shoulder wings) and epaulettes of their red coats. Yellow in varying shades was by far the most popular facing colour of the British army, accounting for some thirty-eight of the one-hundred and eleven regiments known to have been given facing colours. Of all these, some fourteen regiments wore lemon yellow facings similar to that of the 59th. The number 59 was mounted in the various regimental headdresses and on cast into metal coat buttons.

Headquarters was first based in Manchester but moved to Gloucester in March 1756 as recruitment was much more successful in that county and in Somerset. By May, ten companies had been formed and the regiment was posted to Gibraltar under their lemon yellow colours with the number 59 in a red coloured round at the centre. During the regiment's long journey to Gibraltar the British garrison at Minorca was attacked by the French. This effectively began the so called 'Seven Years War' with France. When the 59th arrived at Gibraltar they were immediately sent to Minorca to relieve the British garrison there, but while en route they discovered the island had already surrendered. The 59th returned to Gibraltar where they were stationed for the remainder of the Seven Years War without entering into significant action, although tragically some 107 men died of various illnesses during their stay. At the end of 1756, Ensign William Townshend was killed during fighting with the Spanish over their refusal to surrender a British ship brought into port by a French crew at Algeciras. William Townshend was the first of the regiment to be killed in action.

In early 1757 the regiment was renumbered the 57th due to the disbandment of the 50th and 51st regiments mentioned earlier. At the end of the war with France in 1763, the 57th was one of three regiments sent to re-take possession of Minorca where they were to remain on garrison duty for some time.

After a fairly uneventful five years on the island, the regiment was sent to Ireland where it remained at various locations on civil duties from May 1768 until early 1776. On 12th February 1776, the regiment embarked for America in three ships; the 'Ann & Isabella', the 'Earl of Orford' and the 'Manuel' and eventually arrived at Cape Fear in North Carolina some nine weeks later.

They remained in America playing their part in the War of Independence until 1781, and were involved in the landing on Long Island, The Battle of Brooklyn, Howe's expedition to Chesapeake, The Battle of Brandywine, the Capture of Charlestown and the fall of Yorktown. In 1782, for reasons unknown, the Regiment was renamed the "57th (West Middlesex) Regiment of Foot" and in 1783 was sent to Nova Scotia. The regiment remained stationed there at

Halifax for about eight years. The 57th returned to England, landing at Portsmouth on 14th November 1791 after a two week journey by sea. This was the first time the regiment had been in England since it left for Gibraltar in 1756 some thirty-five years earlier. The regiment was returned to full strength with 22 sergeants, 10 drummers and the minimum number of rank and file – which was 300 at the time. Among the men were 148 English, 139 Scottish, 68 Irish and 9 foreigners. Sixteen of the officers were Scottish, six were English and five were Irish. The regiment spent two years in England, initially stationed at Hilsea near Portsmouth, then in Chesterfield, Loughborough and Tynemouth being used to suppress riots and to prevent smuggling. This domestic duty lasted only a short time, as war with France broke out again in 1793. A previously agreed Anglo-Dutch treaty forced Britain into another war following a French invasion of Holland and British forces quickly began to arrive on the continent. Much of the military activity was directed by politicians in London at this time, which caused huge problems in logistics, troop deployment and the adoption of a useful and practical strategy.

The 57th marched to Edinburgh via Berwick and then sailed from Leith to Portsmouth. From there they travelled to Ostend in Belgium where they arrived on 14th September. The 57th was involved in the relief of Nieuport which had already been taken by the French. Due to preparations for their planned deployment to the West Indies the 57th returned to England. In December 1793, the regiment was shipped back to France to aid French Royalists in La Vendee, but due to transport delays they arrived too late to take part in any action. They were then based at Guernsey for a month or so before returning to England.

With the war being directed by militarily incompetent politicians in London, they could not decide whether to keep the 57th in England, in case of a French invasion threat or to send them to the West Indies as was previously planned. The outcome was that upon their return to England, the 57th were kept onboard their transport ships off Southampton docks and on the Isle of Wight for months waiting for a decision. Typhus claimed forty lives onboard the overcrowded ships from the 57th Regiment alone. Eventually realising their mistake, the government agreed for the men to be allowed to encamp on dry land with fresh water and a ready supply of food. By June 1794, the war in Europe was going very badly for the Allies with both the Austrians and the British suffering heavy losses and being forced to make a massive retreat. The 57th were sent back from England across the Channel to help the Austrians against the French and to defend Ostend at any cost. When they arrived, the Austrians were already beaten and there was no point in fighting further to regain Ostend. The British had to retreat eastward, cross country all the way to the boarder with Holland.

The Austrians having been hammered by the French, now offered no assistance and left the defence of the Netherlands to the British and Dutch forces – so much for going to their aid! The 57th remained in the Netherlands but were poorly supplied and had insufficient equipment and clothing for the colder months. With the British continuing their retreat into Holland and by now abandoned by the Dutch and Austrians, the British Government eventually decided to pull all their troops including the 57th out of the continent. After two months in England, the 57th were sent back to France to help French Royalists in Brittany, but again the transport was delayed and this offered no benefit on the continent after all.

In September 1795, the 57th prepared to sail to the West Indies in order to protect British trade and possessions in that part of the world. They set sail from Portsmouth on 15th November but the transport ships were dashed by a violent storm in the English Channel from which they were forced to return to port. A second attempt was made using three smaller ships, and of these, two were again forced back to Portsmouth by a raging tempest. Eventually the weather broke and a successful journey was accomplished. The whole regiment arrived in the West Indies during May 1796 and immediately set about the repossession of St Lucia, which had been captured by French forces.

Once this was secured, the 57th were sent to Grenada to deal with a local rebellion, which they overcame on 18th June with limited casualties on both sides. Whilst the 57th was highly successful against the French and the rebels in the West Indies, there was a more dangerous enemy in wait for them. As many as 549 succumbed to the effects of Yellow Fever in 1796 and a further 149 died of this the following year.

Now badly undermanned, the regiment was sent to Trinidad to form part of the island garrison. The 57th remained there for around six years without entering into significant action. In May 1803, the regiment returned to England. Of the 350 or so men who arrived back home, some 131 men were immediately discharged as unfit for service. The regiment stayed in England to concentrate on recruitment and training until April 1804, when it was posted to the Guernsey in the Channel Islands. Thomas Norris joined the 57th during this period of recruitment in England. In November 1804, the 57th was sent to Gibraltar until the summer of 1809 at which time they embarked for Lisbon to play their part in the Peninsula War through Portugal, Spain and eventually into France. The 57th's sister regiment the 77th East Middlesex Regiment (of Mysore and Seringaptam fame) had seen service in India and upon return from their expedition to Walcheren and later service in Jersey, they too joined the Peninsula Campaign in 1811. The 77th uniform facings were also yellow, but of a brighter shade.

The 57th were present at; Bussaco, Albuhera (La Albuera), Badajoz, Vittoria, The Pyrenees, Nivelle,

Nive, Toulouse and Aire, although they did not enter into fighting at Busacco and Badajoz and were part of a remote decoy manoeuvre at Toulouse rather than being involved in the main offensive. Their involvement at Bussaco, Badajoz and Toulouse were not deemed sufficient to share in the formal honours. The 77th were present at; El Boden, Cuidad Rodrigo and the 3rd Seige of Badajoz.

In June 1814, at the end of the Peninsula War, the 57th were sent to Canada to prevent American incursions into that country and in August 1814 the 77th were sent to Ireland as a long term posting.

In August 1815, the 57th returned to France after fourteen months, to assist in the final conflict with Napoleon at Waterloo, but arrived too late to take part. In 1816 at the end of the Napoleonic Wars, the 57th and 77th were both given regimental honours to acknowledge their outstanding services in the Peninsula. These honours were then authorised to be included in the respective regimental badges and insignia. The new West Middlesex Regiment badge comprised the number 57 surrounded by laurels with a crown above and a regimental honour scroll with the word 'ALBUHERA' beneath. The pre-1881 army issues of 'Glengarry' type brass badges are an excellent example of this design and are truly beautiful pieces to collect. The new East Middlesex Regiment badge comprised the number 77, again surrounded by laurels, but with the Prince of Wales's Feathers and the motto "Ich Dein" (I serve) above a regimental honour scroll bearing the word 'PENINSULA'. The Prince of Wales's feathers were previously recognised and associated with the 77th regiment on 24th February 1810 and had been unofficially used for some years prior to that.

The 57th remained in France for about three years as part of the army of occupation until November 1818, when they were sent to Ireland. The 77th were stationed at home in England from November 1820, returning to Ireland in June 1823. From 1824 to 1853, the 57th served in Australia, India, England, Ireland and Corfu. The 77th saw service in Jamaica, England, Scotland, Ireland, Malta, Corfu, Canada, Varna and Bulgaria during the same period. Both regiments arrived in the Crimea in September 1854, with the 77th seeing their first action at the Battle of Alma.

The 57th and 77th fought alongside each other at the battle of Inkerman on 5th November the same year and went on to fight together again at Sevastopol in 1855. From 1856 to 1880, the 57th served in Malta, India, Egypt, New Zealand, England, Ireland, Ceylon, and South Africa, taking part in the Maori War of 1863/1866 and the Zulu War in 1879. The 77th regiment served in Ireland, India, England and Burma in the same period and became the 'Duke of Cambridge's Own' on 20th June 1876. In May 1873 both regiments established a depot at Woolwich, which moved to Hounslow in September 1876.

On 1st July 1881, the two regiments along with the Royal Elthorne and Royal East Middlesex Militias were amalgamated to form "The Duke of Cambridge's Own (Middlesex Regiment)", with the 57th forming the first battalion and the 77th forming the second. The new regimental badge was the design we now see in the form of the WW1 Middlesex Regiment cap badge, combining elements of both the earlier 57th and 77th badges. In this design, the Prince of Wales's feathers and the 'Ich Dien' motto sit above an Anglo-Saxon crown with the Duke of Cambridge's cipher and honour scroll bearing the word 'Albuhera'. The whole is surrounded with laurels and below is a ribbon with the words 'Middlesex Regt'.

From 1881, the first battalion were stationed in Ireland, Guernsey, Dover, and Aldershot, returning to Ireland in 1888. In 1892, they were sent to Gibraltar then returned to England in 1895. From England they were posted to South Africa the following year and then to India in 1898. The second battalion served in India at various stations until at least 1893. On 14th January 1897, a draft of men from the first battalion were shipwrecked off Reunion Island in the Indian Ocean, about 430 miles east of Madagascar on their way from South Africa to India. Through strict discipline they somehow, thankfully, managed to survive. The regiment served in the Boer War from 1899 to 1902 where it won two further battle honours, these being *"South Africa"* and *"Relief of Ladysmith"*.

From the turn of the century to the beginning of the First World War, the regiment swelled enormously – firstly due to the activity in South Africa and then due to the imperial arms race designed to prevent a war in Europe. This was achieved by increasing recruitment and adding territorial, volunteer and allied battalions. Of course as history has shown us, the arms race theory did not work in practice and Britain was once again forced to go to war in Europe in 1914. At its largest during the First World War, the Middlesex Regiment numbered a total of 46 battalions.

The regiment went on to win battle honours for their 1914-1918 service at;

"Mons", *"Marne"*, *"Ypres"*, *"Albert"*, *"Bezentin"*, *"Cambrai"*, *"Hindenburg Line"*, *"Suvla"*, *"Jerusalem"*and *"Mesopotamia"*.

The Middlesex Regiment also took part in First World War actions at; Le Cateau, Retreat from Mons, Aisne, La Bassee, Messines, Armentieres, Neuve Chapelle, Gravenstafel, St Julien, Frazenberg, Bellewaarde, Aubers, Hooge, Loos, Somme, Deville Wood, Pozieres, Ginchy, Flers-Courcelette, Morval, Thiepval, Le Transloy, Ancre Heights, Ancre, Bapaume, Arras, Vimy, Scarpe, Arleux, Pilckem, Langemarck, Menin Road, Polygon Wood, Broodseinde, Poelcapelle, Paschendaele, St Quentin, Rosieres, Avre, Villers, Bretonnaux, Lys, Estaires, Hazebrouck, Bailleul, Kemmel, Scherpenberg, Canal du Nord, St Quentin

Canal, Courtrai, Selle, Valenciennes, Sambre, France and Flanders, Italy, Struma, Doiran, Macedonia, Landing at Suvla, Scimitar Hill, Gallipoli, Rumani, Egypt, Gaza, El Mughar, Jericho, Jordan, Tell Asur, Palestine, Murman, Dakhovskaya and Siberia.

In all, the Middlesex Regiment lost a total of 12,694 men of all ranks in what had become known as the "Great War". By the end of the Great War, the British Empire had lost a total of 908,000 servicemen and 31,000 civilians. Britain and her allies eventually emerged victorious over the Germans, who entered a period of hyperinflation due to the immense reparations demanded by the other European nations.

It would not be long before the Germans would attempt a second domination of Europe, spurred by the defeat of the Great War and the humiliation over the payment of reparations which were forcibly taken from them.

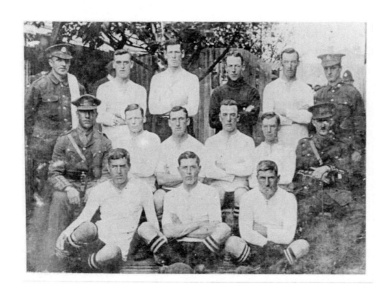

Middlesex Regiment Football Team c1917. Photo from author's collection.

At the end of the First World War, the Middlesex battalions were gradually disbanded as they arrived home, until only four battalions remained. The third battalion was stationed at Aldershot until 1922 and the fourth battalion served in Gibraltar and Egypt for the same duration returning to England itself in 1922. The third and fourth battalions were then disbanded later that year. The first battalion stayed in France until May 1919, then returned to England to the Depot at Mill Hill – which I believe is now known as Inglis Barracks. They soon returned to the continent and were stationed in Cologne until October 1923, when they then travelled back home to England and were also stationed at Aldershot. In 1927 the first battalion were posted to Hong Kong until December 1928, then to Palestine and on to Singapore, returning to Hong Kong in the lead up to the Second World War. The second battalion toured India until 1930 and returned to England being stationed at Colchester from 1931 to 1935 and remaining in England until the outbreak of War in 1939.

During the Second World War, the Middlesex Regiment won battle honours for their 1939–1945 service at;

"Dunkirk", "Normandy Landing", "Caen", "Mont Pincon", "Rhine", "El Alamein", "Akarit", "Sicily", "Anzio" and "Hong Kong".

The regiment also took part in actions at; Dyle, Defence of Escout, Ypres-Comines Canal, Cambes, Breville, Odon, Orne, Hill 112, Bourguebus Ridge, Troarn, Falise, Seine 1944, Nederrijin, Le Harve, Lower Maas, Venraij, Meijel, Geilkirchen, Venlo Pocket, Rhineland, Reichswald, Goch, Lingen, Brinkum, Bremen, North West Europe, Advance on Tripoli, Mareth, Djebel Roumana, North Africa, Francofonte, Sferro, Sferro Hills, Carroceto, Gothic Line, Monte Grande, Italy and South East Asia.

By the end of the war, some 403,000 servicemen and servicewomen along with 92,700 UK civilians were killed.

The Middlesex Regiment saw active service in the Korean War during the early 1950's (as did my late Uncle Brian Norris who co-researched this book) and were awarded a battle honour for their service at *"Nak-tong Bridgehead"*, as well as for the *"Korea"* campaign. The regiment also saw action at; Chongju, Chongchon II, Chaum-ni, Kapyong-Chon, and Kapyong during their time in Korea.

On 31st December 1966, the Middlesex Regiment was amalgamated with:

- The Queen's Royal Surrey Regiment,
- The Queen's Own Buffs (The Royal Kent Regiment) and the
- Royal Sussex Regiment

to form The Queen's Regiment. Interestingly, records show that the 'Surreys' and the 'Buffs' fought alongside the West Middlesex at Albuhera and so once again our regiment found itself in good company. These forebear regiments each have a complex history of development themselves.

The Queen's Royal Surrey Regiment (1st Battalion of the Queens Regiment) had previously been formed in 1959 by amalgamating the Queen's Royal Regiment (The West Surrey) with the East Surrey Regiment. These in turn were previously made up of the old Queen's Royal Regiment and the 31st & 70th of Foot.

The Queen's Own Buffs The Royal Kent Regiment (2nd Battalion of the Queen's Regiment) had only been formed five years earlier in 1961 by amalgamation of The Buffs (Royal East Kent Regiment formed in 1935) and The Queen's Own Royal West Kent Regiment, (formed in 1881). Again these regiments were themselves born out of the old 3rd, 50th and 97th Regiments of Foot.

The Royal Sussex Regiment (3rd Battalion of the Queen's Regiment) had been an 1881 amalgamation of the old 35th of Foot (later the Royal Sussex Regiment) and the 107th Bengal Infantry Regiment.

The addition of the Middlesex Regiment created a 4th Battalion for the Queen's Regiment. The badge of this new regiment retained the Middlesex's Prince of Wales's feathers, which was placed above the Buff's dragon and surrounded by a sword belt with the words "Honi Soit Qui Mal y Pense" from the old Royal Sussex Regiment badge meaning "shame to he who thinks evil of it". Beneath this was placed a scroll with the word "Queen's" to acknowledge the Queen's Royal Surrey Regiment – thus incorporating elements of all four of the forebear regiments in the new badge design. However, the common use of "Duke of Cambridge's Own" and "Middlesex Regiment" in reference to the 4th battalion was removed completely on 1st July 1968 (a month before I was born) and the 4th battalion was reduced to "Albuhera Company" in January 1971.

Sadly in 1973, Albuhera Company, the last remains of the Middlesex Regiment, was disbanded after 218 years of honourable service, leaving behind a proud and glorious history. Numerous battle honours were won during its existence, as were eleven Victoria Crosses and a single George Cross. The Queen's Regiment went on to serve in Ireland on counter terrorism operations, West Germany as part of NATO forces and in Cyprus with the United Nations.

On 9th September, 1992, the remaining battalions of The Queen's Regiment amalgamated with the Royal Hampshire Regiment to create the Princess Of Wales's Royal Regiment (Queen's and Royal Hampshires). The Royal Hampshire Regiment itself was formed in 1946 out of the Hampshire Regiment which combined the 37th and 67th of Foot (North and South Hampshires) in 1881. The badge of the current regiment (PWRR) is similar to that of the previous Queen's Regiment, but with a Tudor style rose placed beneath the dragon and the words "Princess of Wales's" on the scroll below instead of "Queen's". The rose was part of the previous Royal Hampshire Regiment badge, which is a reference to the 37th of Foot's battle of Minden on 1st August, 1759, when on returning from the battle they picked roses and wore them in their headdresses. The custom of wearing the Minden Rose is still preserved in the traditions of the regiment on the 1st August each year. Thus each and every forebear regiment is proudly and cleverly represented in the modern Princess of Wales's Royal Regiment badge.

The Silent Toast

Another important custom strictly observed by the regiment is The Silent Toast, made to "the immortal memory of the Die Hards" on Albuhera Day, 16th May each year. Originally instituted by the sergeants of the 57th, the day after the battle of Albuera (as so few officers remained), this is traditionally made in the Sergeant's mess, in honour of those who fell. All participants stand shoulder to shoulder in a circle, with any women present being supported by a man on either side. A large pewter tankard with the number "57" and the words "to the immortal memory" inscribed upon it is filled with red wine or other suitable alcoholic beverage. The most senior man (with the most junior man to his immediate right) calls for silence and takes a drink from the tankard, then passes it clockwise to the next person, who also takes a drink and passes it on. The tankard is passed around the circle for all to drink in silence and eventually it reaches the last person, who is of course the most junior man. Before he drinks, the others in the circle say the words "and the rest" and the junior man is expected to drink down the remaining contents of the tankard, however much there is remaining.

A book is normally kept to record the silent toast each year which everyone signs as the final part of the custom. My brother Paul and I took part in the silent toast for the first time on 14th May 2005, with members of the Middlesex Regiment, senior military representatives from Spain and Portugal and the Friends of the British Cemetery at Elvas. We explained the silent toast to our Spanish friends at the Campamento Festero in La Albuera, and this has become part of the tradition on the anniversary of the battle there too.

The Princess of Wales's Royal Regiment (PWRR) remains the county infantry regiment of Kent, Surrey, Sussex, Middlesex, Hampshire, The Isle of Wight and the Channel Islands. Headquarters are now at Howe Barracks in Canterbury, Kent.

Middlesex Regiment and Princess of Wales's Royal Regiment representatives at the Chapel of St John (San Juan) at Elvas in Portugal, where those lost in the Battle of Albuera and the Storming of Badajoz are buried. Photograph taken 15th May, 2004.

Colonels of The Regiment

27/12/1755	Lt Col John Arabin
16/2/1757	Sir David Cunynhame
4/11/1767	Sir John Irwin
2/11/1780	General John Campbell
8/9/1806	General John Hely-Hutchinson, 2nd Earl of Donoughmore.
27/4/1811	General Sir H.W.Whitford Dalrymple Bt.
4/10/1830	General Sir William Inglis KCB.
4/12/1835	General Sir Frederick Adam GCB, GCMG.
31/5/1843	Sir Henry Hardinge, 1st Viscount Hardinge GCB.
24/9/1856	General Sir James Frederick Love GCB, KH.
5/9/1865	General Charles Richard Fox.
14/4/1873	General Freeman Murray.
11/12/1875	General Sir Edward Alan Holdich GCB.
1881	General Sir Edward Alan Holdich GCB. (1st Batt)
	General Harry Hope Graham CB. (2nd Batt)
24/3/1897	General Sir George Harry Smith Willis GCB.
30/11/1900	Lt-Gen Henry Kent.
25/2/1921	General Sir Ivor Maxse KCB,CVO, DSO.
10/5/1932	Brig-Gen Ronald Macclesfield Heath CMG, DSO.

22/4/1942	Colonel Maurice Browne MC.
22/4/1952	Lt- Gen Gerard Corfield Bucknall CB, MC.
1/8/1959	Major-General Sir John E. F. Willoughby KBE,CB.
31/12/1966	Lt-General Sir Richard Craddock.
31/12/1977	Major-General Rowland Spencer Noel Mans CBE.
1/1/1984	Brig Herbert Charles Millman OBE
Jan 1989	Major-General Michael Frank Reynolds.
9/9/1992	Lt-General Sir Anthony Denison-Smith KBE
9/9/1999	Brig E.R. Holmes CBE, TD.

Regimental Marches:

Most British regiments have (or have had) their own regimental music to march to, which distinguishes them from other regiments on parade and at official events. The Middlesex's First Battalion march is "The Sir Manley Power" and the Second Battalion march is known as "Paddy's Resource". These were re-written and combined by Band Master J.E.Thirtle when the two battalion bands joined. The combined march was approved as the official Middlesex Regimental March in 1950, by His Majesty King George VI.

Middlesex Regiment - Peninsula War Battles:

Battle	Date(s)	57th present	77th present	Notes
Bussaco	26-27 Sept 1809	Yes	No	57th remained in reserve and not brought in to action. Battle Honours not bestowed.
Albuhera	16 May 1811	Yes	No	Principal Battle Honour of the Middlesex Regiment . Thomas Norris involved and awarded clasp with MGS Medal in 1848.
El Boden	25 Sept 1811	No	Yes	77th famous rear guard action
Cuidad Rodrigo	9 – 19/ Jan 1812	No	Yes	77th involved taking the fortress.
Badajoz	16 March – 6 April 1812	No	Yes	57th as covering army, 77th in action during storming of fortress.
Vittoria	21 June 1813	Yes	No	Thomas Norris involved and awarded clasp with MGS Medal in 1848.
Pyrenees	25 July – 2 Aug 1813	Yes	No	Thomas Norris involved and awarded clasp with MGS Medal in 1848.
Nivelle	10 Nov 1813	Yes	No	Thomas Norris involved and awarded clasp with MGS Medal in 1848.
Nive	9 -13 Dec 1813	Yes	No	Thomas Norris involved and awarded clasp with MGS Medal in 1848.
Aire	2 March 1814	Yes	No	Thomas Norris involved
Toulouse	10 April 1814	Yes	No	57th not involved in main attack on Toulouse, so Battle Honours not bestowed.

214

Remembrance Day 2004

9. Remembrance Day 2004

As mentioned in chapter 3, Paul and I forged good relationships with many members of the Middlesex Regiment during our brief visit to La Albuera in May, 2004. We swapped contact details with several of them and corresponded by post & email throughout the remainder of the year. I wrote to our new friends to tell them about the book I was writing and this generated further interest in our story.

In October, Paul and I were kindly invited to attend the annual Remembrance Day service at Inglis Barracks in Mill Hill, and we keenly accepted. We arrived on Sunday 14th November sporting our Middlesex Regiment blazers and ties, along with my daughter Sadie (aged 9) and my Son Alfie (aged 4). Gerry Patmore's familiar face greeted us when we made our way through the stringent security and approached the chapel entrance. As bearer of the Middlesex Regimental colours, he was decked out in full regalia – gauntlets and all. Gerry and his comrades quietly welcomed us in and we were ushered to seats at the rear of the congregation. After a thought provoking sermon, which made several references to the plight of our forces in Iraq and those lost there in recent months, we made our way solemnly outside.

The various regiments and corps in attendance began to fall in and Gerry asked for formal permission for Paul and I to take part in the planned parade, along with him and the rest of the Middlesex contingent. The senior officer agreed, although with my children present, both Paul and I could not march together – one of us would have to look after the children. Paul graciously stood down and insisted that I join the march while he watched the parade with Sadie and Alfie. I stood in line with the other Middlesex men, three files deep. In all about two hundred of us of various corps marched from the chapel to the barracks war memorial only a few hundred yards away. Local dignitaries, and incumbent commanding officers laid poppy wreathes as a mark of respect.

Stirring words were spoken in remembrance of those who fought in the past and in honour of those who are now on active service abroad. A period of silence was perfectly observed following these formalities and the quietness was only broken by the sound of a rousing bugle.

Following this, the parade, myself included, continued to march around the memorial and back down to the chapel where we had started. Luckily, Paul had packed his camera and captured some good images of the parade which I have included here. This was a wonderful experience, having never marched before and this was the first time in 189 years that one of our line has marched with the regiment. The last time would have been just before Thomas was invalided out of the 57th of foot in November 1816.

Remembrance Day 2004 at Mill Hill.
Gerry Patmore bearing the Middlesex Regiment Colours.

*Monument to 12,694 members of the Middlesex
Regiment who lost their lives during the course of the
Great War.*

Re-enactment

10. Re-enactment

During the time I have spent studying uniform designs, muskets and military accessories of the Napoleonic period I have relied heavily on specialists with particular knowledge in respect of materials, fabrication and use. Many of these specialists make and supply an ever growing number of Napoleonic re-enactment regiments and period enthusiasts throughout Britain, Europe, North America and even Australia. They specialise in making shakos, coatees, trousers muskets, swords, daggers, bayonets, buckles, boots, ammunition boxes, leather works, badges, buttons, water canisters, gaiters and any other item you might possibly wish to have, in order to create an authentic copy of a period uniform and kit. I myself wanted to have a full 57th West Middlesex Regiment uniform made, complete with shako, musket and all the various accessories as would have been worn by Thomas Norris at the battle of Albuera in 1811. I intended to wear the uniform during the annual parade on 16th May at Albuera and to take part in one of the re-enactments with my brother Paul. I wasn't sure it would be possible to produce such a uniform to begin with. First I had to find out the exact uniform details – particularly for the coatee and shako. Much of this information is captured in military artwork, but this needed to be precise. I found some uniform information in books at the local library and in others which I purchased in the high street and on the Internet. I carried out a web search to find some local contacts and to my delight, I stumbled across the Napoleonic Association (NA) website.

The NA provided several re-enactment contacts in England, and before long, with help from Jim Harlow, Ron Bridgehouse, Rob Anderson, Ed Parker and Ann Belsey I was well on the way to building up a precise specification for my 57th uniform. Ron even managed to have some 57th belt plates made up by taking a mould from an old original piece he came across. The Sutler's Stores in Bournemouth were commissioned to make the coatee, trousers and leather work, and Kitty Hats of High Wycombe were asked to make a stovepipe shako. Rob Anderson of the 88th Connaught Rangers also kindly created a shako for my trip to Spain. Other accessories and accoutrements such as gaiters and water canteens etc… were provided by Jim Harlow of the 3rd of Foot (The Buffs) to bring the whole thing together.

57th West Middlesex Regiment uniform of 1811.

Now I needed to know how to march. Well I'd had a bash at it on Remembrance Day at Mill Hill with Gerry Patmore, but didn't feel very confident. The last thing I wanted to do having gone to all the trouble of getting a uniform made, was to do an impression of "Stupid Boy Pyke" on parade at La Albuera and at the command turn and march off in the wrong direction. To aid the prevention of such an embarrassing eventuality, I enlisted the help of Napoleonic expert Jim Harlow, who along with a hand-full of other Napoleonic re-enactors kindly showed me the basics of musket drilling and marching. I seemed to pick it up after a while and felt that with practice, I should just about get by in La Albuera.

Napoleonic drill is very different to that of the modern day, particularly when presenting arms. In Napoleonic times, presenting arms was precisely that – presenting the firing mechanism of your musket for inspection, thus the fire lock faces away from the soldier, so the inspecting officer can easily see it.

Muskets and Rifles.

As mentioned in chapter 5, British infantry soldiers like Thomas were equipped with smooth bore East India pattern Brown Bess muskets during the Napoleonic period. The musket used a flintlock or firelock mechanism to propel a lead ball at high speed, which basically worked like a mini hand-held cannon. A small amount of gunpowder from a pre-

prepared paper cartridge was placed in the priming pan on the outside part of the firelock. The pan was then closed and the musket "cast about" to point the barrel upwards. The remainder of the gunpowder in the cartridge was then poured into the barrel from the upper end and a lead ball was then added. The remaining empty cartridge paper was then rolled up and stuffed in to the end of the barrel as wadding, and a ram rod used to push the whole charge down the barrel and compact it. This was known as muzzle loading.

The firelock was then pulled back one notch or "half-cocked" on the firing mechanism. The musket was now loaded, but in a safety mode as if the trigger were to be pulled accidentally, it would only "go off half cocked" and not actually fire the weapon.

When ready, the firelock could be fully cocked and at the command the trigger pulled purposely, releasing the spring-loaded firing mechanism holding a sharpened piece of flint. This would spring forward clockwise about the centre of the firelock and strike the friezen, an upright piece of metal connected to the priming pan. This causes the priming pan cover to open and at the same time creates a friction induced spark. The spark ignites the gunpowder in the priming pan, which flashes and in turn this ignites the main charge in the barrel through a small hole known as a touch hole. The expanding gases released during the explosion in the barrel, force the lead musket ball through it and this basically fires the weapon.

This was quite a lengthy and fairly clumsy process, which was often unreliable, on average failing to fire once in every fifteen shots. When a firelock set off the powder in the priming pan but failed to ignite the main charged, this was known as a "hang fire". Muskets were notoriously inaccurate, even at close range and as mentioned before, soldiers often relied on the use of their 18" bayonets if time was short in close fighting.

Rifle regiments such as the 95th were generally provided with the shorter muzzle loaded Baker Rifles which were far more accurate, given the development of new technology at the time. The Baker Rifle takes its name from Ezekiel Baker, a very well known and respected gun maker of the period who revolutionised the design of firearms. Essentially the 30" rifle barrel has a series of seven groves or "rifles" along the length of its internal surface. When the gun is fired, the ball is forced along the barrel and the rifling causes it to spin very fast. The effect of this is to equalise the air pressure around the ball as it leaves the barrel, thus reducing the effects of drag and wind. This allows the ball to more closely follow its intended course and hopefully to hit the required target (normally a Frenchman). These weapons were loaded and fired in the same way as muskets, although the rifling in the barrel allowed a build up of debris in the groves after a time and riflemen were also issued with wooden mallets in the early days to help them hammer home the ramrod and charge as the debris caused such a tight fit.

Officers usually had pistols rather than rifles, and as they were expected to equip themselves at their own cost when taking up a commission, they would select the size, weight and maker of a pistol, according to the design they liked and the price they were willing to pay. For this reason, officer's pistols are recorded as being of very many different types and sizes during the period.

Exact replicas of these beautiful "black powder" firearms are still used today by the various re-enactment organisations around the world, during public displays and at "Living History" events. In Great Britain, it is a strict legal requirement for anyone owning a musket to possess a full shotgun license and those with pistols must have a fire arms certificate. Re-enactors are keen to re-create events and activities of the past as accurately as possible in the modern day – particularly when involved in television work and teaching. This goes much further than simply having the right uniforms and weaponry.

Many re-enactors strictly observe army rules and regulations set out in the military handbooks of the day which were originally written and imposed in about 1804. There were regulations for everything and each activity the solders were involved in was broken down into easy to follow orders or commands. For example there were a total of twelve separate commands required for a company of men to load and fire their muskets simultaneously, and these are the very orders Thomas would have had to follow many thousands of times during his time in the Peninsula…

1. "By order, prepare to prime and load"
2. "Prime and load"
3. "Handle Cartridge"
4. "Prime your pans"
5. "About" (point mussel upward ready to load)
6. "Withdraw ramrod"
7. "Ram down cartridge"
8. "Replace ramrod"
9. "Attention"
10. "Make Ready"
11. "Present"
12. "Fire"

"Make ready" refers to fully cocking the musket and "present" means to take aim.

Detailed procedures and routines such as this were closely observed by the army and remain an essential safety control in the re-enactment world today. Without such close attention to detail there would be a significant risk of personal injury – particularly in bayonet practice! Fortunately, with these strict controls in place, accidents are a very rare occurrence. The Napoleonic Association arranges national and international events which are generally supported by governments around the world and has a dedicated membership of many thousands of people.

The Victorian Die Hards

Rather uniquely, the 57th have a world class Victorian period re-enactment regiment, which is not surprisingly named "The Die Hards". This group attends events all over the UK and is involved in considerable television and film work throughout the world. They are committed to providing as accurate a portrayal of a Victorian period regiment as possible, fielding members in Crimean War, Zulu War and Boer War uniform recreations. They also have members in WW1 and WW2 Middlesex Regiment uniforms, with all members practicing the drills of each period. I met the Die Hards for the first time at Dover Castle in early July 2005, having been invited by their organiser Tim Rose to join them at the "Spirit of the Regiment" event arranged by the PWRR.

I attended with my 57th Napoleonic period uniform and took part in the public display along with the other Die Hard members. The display ended with a long line of us in chronological order on the parade ground from Napoleonic to Crimean, to Zulu, to Boer, to WW1 and finally to WW2, with me positioned proudly on the right flank (as instructed by the officiating Army Colonel) at the position of honour in my 1811 'Albuhera' kit.

At the order, we all presented arms and the crowd applauded – a very special and unique experience. Having had a brief insight into the world of re-enactment, and having seen the sheer hard work, expense and commitment these people devote to their hobby and love of history, I would be most remiss not to include at least a few of them here in recognition of their undying efforts to keep our nation's proud history alive. Hats or rather "shakos" off to them!

The Die Hards Crimean Company. Note the very different "Albert Shako" and cuff design of the 1850's. This was the last tailed coatee to be worn by British soldiers.

The Die Hards Victorian Home Service Company.
Uniforms reproduced from patterns of the 1870's
and 1880's. Photographs included with kind permission
of the Die Hard Company – see their excellent website
for more information.

6th Portuguese Cacadores at Elvas in Portugal, following their "Black Powder Salute" to those lost in the Battle of Albuhera. Taken May 2005.

The 57th of Foot Re-enactment Regiment of La Albuera in Spain. Picture taken on 16th May 2004 at Wellington Park with Middlesex Regiment veterans in the background.

Researching
Family History

11. Researching Family History

The process can involve some very big numbers. To illustrate, start with a single child, say my son Alfie, and work backwards in time. He has two parents, four grandparents, eight great grand parents, sixteen great, great grandparents, and so on with the number doubling each generation we go back.

This means that by the time of my ancestor John Norris who was born in 1565, Alfie has 4,096 great, great, great, great, great, great, great, great, great grandparents. If you were able to write a list of all these names one below the other, the list would be about 32 metres long (about 105 feet).

If we continue projecting back in time, by 1308 when Sir Jean Norreise came to England, the number of Alfie's direct ancestors passes the million mark. By the Norman Conquest, Alfie has over 133 million direct ancestors, and by the time of Christ, Alfie's direct ancestors total more than five and a half thousand trillion in a single generation. If you were able to write a list of all these names, it would be over 27 billion miles long, which is five times the distance from the Sun to the planet Pluto and back.

Clearly, this mathematical relationship doesn't stand up to scrutiny, as the population has massively increased since the time of Christ! Even thirteenth century records show a total population of only four million people living in England and Wales. This can only mean one thing. At some point as we track back in time, from generation to generation, it can only be that the various families living at any given time were all distantly related to each other, and therefore one person accounts for very many ancestor relationships in our supposed list. All men are therefore truly brothers.

Nowadays, many people put family trees together very quickly using research carried out by other people or by simply making assumptions about who was who and when. Given the various registers of names in each town or county, would-be genealogists can pick and choose to suit themselves and the history they would like. There are professional genealogists who will charge for research services, but they can rarely guarantee the accuracy of the details they sell you.

In a similar way, there are people who try to link names on current electoral registers with fifteenth or sixteenth century nobility. Then they try to flog you a brief history of that family, suggesting that you are distantly related to them – of course, there is never any proof of this relationship. This is all a bit of a racket, and I would deter anyone from purchasing information in this way. The only way to accurately trace your family history is to do it either by yourself or in an organised group and to obtain documentary evidence at each generation, proving lineage beyond any doubt.

The fairly recent introduction of the Internet as a tool for family history research was initially welcomed but has proved to be less and less useful. Again the temptation is to make an assumption about relationships between known ancestors and those details on the Internet that would make a nice fit – not a definite, documented relationship. Many people claim to have researched their family history, but very, very few have actually proven each generation of ancestors. This is precisely what we have done. The ancestors described in this book were real people, who have contributed to the genetic make-up of the living generations of this family. I carry in me a small part of each of them, which I have passed on to my children. An eternal flame if you like, that continues to burn, passing from candle to candle, generation to generation from the beginning of time up to the very moment you read this. In this way, part of us goes on living forever in our descendants. DNA analysis is sometimes used in tracing or rather establishing ancestry, particularly in legal cases, but more recently by linking historic figures with people living now.

This gives a good idea of the geographical spread of a family over time. DNA analysis cannot conclusively prove the paternal line, it can only establish who is not the father of a child, and can only give a percentage likelihood of an individual being the father. As you are probably aware, our genetic code is carried in structures known as chromosomes. Males have what are called 'Y' chromosomes and females have 'X' chromosomes – their names taken from their physical shapes when viewed under electron microscope. The male lacks the fourth leg, which the female has to make it an X. This fourth leg contains mitochondrial DNA, which is passed directly and unchanged from mother to daughter ad infinitum. If we had samples of mitochondrial DNA for the female line going back say seven-hundred years, we would find that the maternal parents in each generation have perfectly matching DNA codes. With this in mind, we can see that only the direct maternal line of female ancestry can ever be proven to 100% accuracy. This scientific method is in support of the common sense view that there can be no certainty about who the father of a child is – only certainty about the mother (from a records point of view), as the mother may not have restricted herself to a single partner.

What is history?

The dawn of history began of course with the invention of writing, which is thought to have occurred around 3100 B.C. in Mesopotamia, only about 400 years after the invention of the wheel. This kind of writing was basically made up of pictographic characters representing the Sumerian spoken language. The earliest decipherable writing is on clay tablets, and consists of lists showing the ownership of jars of oil and bundles of reeds. The invention of writing and therefore 'history' was born out of the necessity to record wealth and possession, in a similar way to the development of mathematics.

As years went by, various alphabets evolved until complex formal scripts could be written. Writing was inspired by the emergence of philosophy and science in ancient Greece, particularly the works of Socrates and Plato. Early books such as Homer's Iliad and the Odyssey moved into poetry and rhythmic hexameter verse, but still the text records historic events and the exchange of possessions. The military campaigns of Alexander the Great in the fifth century B.C, and those of Julius Caesar in the first century B.C. were recorded by historians, and these detailed chronicles provided a model for recording military gains and losses until recent years. Since ancient times, there has been a need to record important events and agreements, in order to prove that such events and agreements have actually occurred and to allocate responsibility to named individuals. Distrust is in our nature.

Identification of individuals was a problem in Britain during the mediaeval period as over half the men in any village or town were named Thomas, Richard or Henry. Most of the others were called William, John, Joseph or James. This is where the term 'any Tom, Dick or Harry' comes from.

Surnames were not used in Britain until after the Norman Conquest and even then, much of the population did not start using Surnames until the thirteenth and fourteenth centuries. Before that, people would identify each other by adding things like 'son' or 's' to their own names, in order to form names for their children. In Scotland, Mc or Mac was used instead of 'son' and 's', and in Ireland, 'O' was used. When things got too complicated as the population increased, they started to add characteristics to their names such as: - physical features (Thomas the Small of Watford), personal qualities (Richard the Wise of Radlett), an individual's occupation (Henry the Carpenter of Abbots Langley) or geographical area (William the Northfield). As time went on, the word 'the' was shortened to 't', and the word 'of' was shortened to 'o', then in most cases removed all together. This mimicked the Norman use of 'de' in their French style names.

Eventually, the Norman fashion of using surnames caught on in England and people had to decide what surname to take on. Most people simply adapted their existing names, then passed this on to their children but pre-fixed it with another first name, usually after a favourite saint. This was known as a "Christian Name".

The Plague

Using surnames had just started to get organised when the Black Death otherwise known as bubonic plague struck in June 1348. The plague entered Britain at Melcombe in Weymouth Bay, Dorset and was carried in the intestines of fleas breeding in the fur of black rats. The Black Death originated in Asia and spread to southern Europe via the spice trading routes. Trade ships then unknowingly carried the disease from Italian ports on the Mediterranean to England, where it infected the population until 1352. Current estimates suggest as much as forty percent of the population died of the plague. In 1349, it claimed an average of three hundred lives a day. In all, about two million of a national population of five million died.

This meant that many of the hereditary titles and surnames developed before that time were lost forever as whole families and lineages were completely wiped out. It took three centuries for the population to recover to its previous level. The plague struck again in 1360-62 and 1369, and remained endemic in Britain until its final outbreak in 1665 which is known to history as "The Great Plague". The plague was eventually halted in and around the capital by the Fire of London the following year - the fire itself destroyed around 13,200 houses over an area of 400 acres. This sudden loss of population makes it very difficult to link families living before the Black Death with those after it, as few records can truly identify exactly which lines of each family surname survived. Hardly any genealogists can continue tracing a direct line beyond that time. All we can do is to find an association of families based on geographical concentrations of people with the same surname and continue tracing the line back from there. All research to accurately and efficiently trace a single line should start with the current generation and work backward in time. Researching in the opposite direction would be very time consuming and costly as records do not lend themselves to being found easily without direction from a later document. (i.e generally a birth will follow a marriage of parents and a death will follow both these events).

Civil Registration Documents

The main records required to begin researching family history are, as you would expect, those relating to births, deaths and marriages. A record of birth is needed to record the father of the child, or at least to apportion responsibility for providing for that child. It is also needed to register the existence of the child for taxation purposes. These birth records are used by the government Office of National Statistics which aids formation of policy on education, employment and social services.

For example, this information will provide an idea of how many schools and teachers will be needed in any given area in say ten years time. A marriage record is needed to register a marriage for tax purposes and to prevent polygamy, which is illegal in this country. It is also to prove the marriage actually occurred and to place responsibility on the husband to provide for his wife and children. Note the marriage certificate is always given to the bride at a wedding ceremony, not to the Bridegroom. A record of death is needed to document the actual or likely cause of death and establish if homicide or suicide have taken place. Both of these actions have legal and financial implications so far as insurance and assurance policies are concerned. It is also needed to prove the individual is no longer living, in order that property may pass into the possession of legitimate heirs and debts to be settled. In addition to this, without a record of death, the Inland Revenue will continue to levy taxes on an individual, and they will remain on the electoral register – and therefore will still be entitled to vote.

You will note that all three documents are primarily required for financial purposes. Certificates of births, deaths and marriages are collectively known as civil registration documents, which have been kept and maintained in England and Wales since about 1836. Civil registration did not fully commence In Scotland until 1855 and in Ireland it was as late as 1864 due to the distinction between Catholics and Protestants – strangely Catholics were not considered important enough to register in those days.

All these records were once stored in Somerset House, then later in St Catherine's House in Holborn. They are now held at the Family Records Centre in Islington, not far from Angel underground Station. Civil registration documents only take us back to my Great, Great Grandparents, which makes tracing earlier ancestors a little more difficult. Beyond 1836, we rely heavily on parish church records. In about 1535, King Henry VIII decreed that in order to accurately tax the population, parish churches had to record all baptisms, marriages and burials in a church register. Until this time, only the nobility and wealthy landed gentry had such events recorded, but the royal decree now applied to everyone. Unfortunately, due to Henry VIII's anti-catholic tendencies, much of the clergy did not obey his wishes and as a result very few parishes actually recorded these events. In most cases, where early records were made, they were destroyed by fire or eaten by vermin and so information from this period is scarce.

In the late 1550's, Queen Elizabeth I re-iterated her father's decree and forcefully ordered that these parish registers be used. As you can imagine, with Elizabeth's famous zero tolerance policy, very few parishes resisted and consequently, a vast pool of information was compiled nationally. Over the years though, many of these records were lost principally during the Great Fire of London in 1666 and the Blitz during World War II. The earliest parish records are written in Latin, others in old English and many are extremely difficult to read and interpret. At one time,

Latin was the only written language used by the educational establishment – particularly those universities providing for the clergy and legal professions.

Many of the records offices are able to offer a transcription service for a small fee and this could save you days in trying to make sense of these very old and delicate documents which are often beautifully hand-written.

Other Sources of Information

Civil registration documents and parish records are often not enough to provide sufficient detail about the individuals being researched. In addition to these sources, we can also extract information from: the IGI (International Genealogical Index), military service records, wills, property deeds, land registry, census returns, Bishops transcripts, manorial rolls, grave stones, cemeteries, pay registers, tax records and family bibles. Most of these are available from Public Records Offices, County Records Offices, local museums and reference libraries throughout the country. The entire 1881 census return is now available on compact disks at a modest cost from the Church of Latter-Day Saints, as are some international baptism, marriage and burial records. The 1901 census return has recently become viewable via the Government's Public Records Office website.

There is a small charge to carry out searches and for downloading copies of the census pages. This saves lots of time in conventional research techniques and is normally much less expensive than travelling to the records office and purchasing copies of the pages you require. Note that Census returns, the document in which census information is completed and returned to the government, are not made available to the public for a period of at least one-hundred years due to data protection legislation. Unfortunately, Uncle Brian and I carried out our research before these electronic and digital information systems were available, and so it took us far more time to complete than it would nowadays.

The best way to start your research is to speak to as many elderly relatives as you can. It is a good idea to prepare a list of questions you would like to ask on a piece of paper to help get the best out of each interview. Try to find out the year and location the individuals you are researching were born and an idea of where they went to school or worked. Names of their siblings and other generations would also be helpful, as would any old photographs you might be able to find. With this very basic information, you can visit the Family Records Centre in Islington and easily look up a reference for a birth registration using the individual's surname along with the district and approximate year of birth. Make sure you check for any duplication. If the birth year information is not available, then try to find a marriage or death registration. Information held on these will give clues to the year of birth and other family names which might help with cross referencing checks to ensure you've got the right person. With all these civil registration certificates, you cannot see the information unless you purchase a copy of the registration for about £6.50 each, ordering them using the forms provided at the FRC in Islington. They usually take a few days to post to you. With the information provided by that certificate you can continually repeat the process looking for births, marriages, deaths and census returns back to the early Victorian period.

Once those resources are exhausted, I would suggest the next port of call should be the County Records Office for parish records. Be warned, this is very hard and tiring work, which can take long hours and sometimes days to complete searches for a single document. Many of the records, particularly the Parish Registers are kept on microfiche or microfilm, which can be studied and photo-copied from viewing machines fitted with lenses and back-lighting. This is an excellent way of providing public access to copies of the records and obviously helps to preserve the originals. It can be very hard on the eyes though, so it is a good idea to plan different types of research during each visit to the records centres in order to break the monotony and allow your eyes to rest periodically. In my experience, putting in the time and effort is well worth while. However, it is only when you discover a particularly illusive piece of information that you realise your addiction to this kind of research and find yourself clenching your fist and shouting "yessss!" in some quiet corner of a library somewhere. It all sounds a bit sad doesn't it? But, it really has been quite rewarding as I have learned so much and met so many amazing people.

I wish you the very best of luck with any research you might decide to carry out yourself and hope these few pages can provide some direction and assistance. Stick with it.

Timeline Reference

12. Timeline Reference
Historic events during Thomas's lifetime

1778 - Thomas Norris born in Watford.
      - Population of Watford is around 2000
      - Catholic Relief Act – Catholics now allowed
          places of worship
      - William Pitt (Senior) dies aged 69.
1780 - Anti-Catholic riots in London.
      - Britain declares war on the Netherlands.
1782 - First use of Eagle on US State seal.
1783 - Treaty of Versailles between Britain, France
          and the USA
      - Britain recognises independence of
          American colonies.
      - First ascent of a manned hot air balloon.
1785 - Power loom invented by Edmund
          Cartwright.
1787 - First convicts sent to Botany Bay, New South
          Wales.
1788 - Death of Bonnie Prince Charlie aged 67.
1789 - Fall of the Bastille in France.
      - Declaration of the Rights of Man.
1791 - Mozart dies in Vienna
      - George Washington elected first President of
          the United States.
1792 - British warship "Royal George" capsizes
          killing 900 men.

1793 - France declares war against Britain and
        Holland.
1794 - Theatre Royal opens in Drury Lane, London.
1796 - Jenner discovers safe vaccine for small pox.
1798 - Irish Rebellion
1799 - Battle of Seringaptam
     - Moses Norris, Thomas's brother dies in
        Watford.
1800 - Union of Britain and Ireland.
     - Female life expectancy in Britain is around 35
        years
     - Population of London is about one million
1801 - Nelson's battle of Copenhagen – Danish fleet
        destroyed.
     - Thomas Norris found guilty of stealing two
        loaves of bread.
     - Population of Watford is around 2300
     - Davy Lamp invented
1802 - The Factory Act
     - Thomas Norris marries Ann Buck at Henley-
        on-Thames.
1803 - Britain declares war on France.
     - Thomas Norris joins the West Middlesex
        Regiment,
1804 - Napoleon Bonaparte made Emperor in
        France.
     - Richard Trevithick invents the first steam
        locomotive engine to run on rail tracks.
     - Telford begins construction of Caledonian
        Canal
1805 - Nelson's battle of Trafalgar against France
        and Spain. Nelson is killed.

- Russia and Austria defeated by French at Austerlitz. Napoleon is master of Europe.
1807 - British Parliament moves to abolish the slave trade.
- French troops cross into Spain and Portugal.
- Gas lighting installed at Pall Mall, London.
1808 - Joseph Bonaparte installed as King of Spain.
- British forces arrive in Portugal. Battles of Vimiero and Rolica.
- British drive French out of Portugal.
- British retreat to Corunna and leave the Peninsula.
1809 - British return to Portugal under Sir Arthur Wellesley.
- Battle of Talavera, British victorious over the French.
- Thomas Norris enters the Peninsula War with the 57th.
- Birth of Charles Darwin.
1810 - Battle of Bussaco.
1811 - Battle of Albuera, British victory over French in Spain.
- King George III confined to Windsor. Prince George becomes Regent.
- Battle of El Boden
1812 - Charles Dickens is born.
- Seige of Cuidad Rodrigo – British take strategic city.
- Seige of Badajoz – 77th involved in storming the fortress.

1813 - Battle of Vittoria – British victorious over
French.
- Battles of the Pyrenees – British push French
out of Iberia.
- Battles of Nive and Nivelle – British victories
in France.
1814 - Burial in woollen shrouds no longer required
by law
- Battle of Aire
- Battle of Toulouse
- Napoleon abdicates and is exiled to the
island of Elba
1815 - Napoleon escapes from Elba and returns to
France.
- Thomas Norris service in Canada.
- Battle of Waterloo, Napoleonic Wars are
ended
- Chelsea Hospital now has 36,757 Out-
Pensioners
- Thomas's daughter Sarah baptised on 12th
May at Watford.
1816 - Photography invented.
- Thomas Norris leaves army service at
Valenciennes.
1818 - Grand Union Canal under construction
through Herts
- Thomas's son David baptised on 12th April at
Watford.
1819 - Thomas's daughter Mary born in Watford.
- Thomas Norris recalled to 7th Royal
Veterans Battalion.
1820 - George IV crowned King of England.

- Spanish revolution begins.
- Thomas Norris' son William is born in Jersey.
- Electro-magnetism discovered by Hans Oersted
- Enclosure of open fields completed (started 1750)
1821 - Death of Napoleon Bonaparte.
1822 - Death of poet Percy Shelley.
1823 - William Sturgeon invents the electric motor
- Thomas Norris Discharged from 7th Royal Veterans Battalion.
1824 - Death of Lord Byron, English poet.
- Royal National Lifeboat Institution (RNLI) established.
1825 - Stockton to Darlington public railway opened.
- Trade Unions legalised.
1828 - Duke of Wellington becomes Prime Minister.
1829 - Robert Peel founds Metropolitan Police.
1830 - King George IV dies of cirrhosis at Windsor Castle.
- William IV crowned King of England.
- Rainhill Locomotive Trials – Stevenson's "Rocket" wins.
1831 - Discovery of magnetic north pole by Captain John Ross.
1833 - Great Britain abolishes slavery throughout the Empire.
- Employment of children under the age of 9 prohibited by law
1834 - Poor Law Act in England.

1835 - West Coast Main Line Railway under
             construction through Watford.
       - First telegraph experiments conducted by
             Samuel Morse
1836 - Civil Registration begins in England and
             Wales
       - Mexicans storm the Alamo.
       - Watford Railway Station is opened
1837 - King William IV dies of pneumonia and liver
             failure.
       - Queen Victoria crowned on 20th June aged
             eighteen.
1838 - Population of Watford is 2,960
1839 - First Henley Regatta.
       - Tea first imported to UK from India.
       - Steam Hammer invented by James Nasmyth
1840 - Penny postage introduced in Britain.
       - Opium War between Britain and China.
       - Dr David Livingstone travels to Africa.
       - Queen Victoria marries Prince Albert of Sax-
             Coburg.
1841 - First full National Census in England & Wales
1842 - Rotherhithe tunnel under Thames is opened.
       - Hong Kong ceded to Britain by China.
1843 - Charles Dickens publishes "A Christmas
             Carol"
1844 - YMCA founded in London.
       - First message sent by electric telegraph.
1845 - Failed potato crop in Ireland causes the
             Great Famine.
       - US annexes Texas.
1846 - The Planet Neptune discovered.

1848   - Gold discovered in California.
       - Queen Victoria sets the tradition of the
           English family Christmas with
           Christmas tree and presents.
       - Military General Service Medal issued for
           1793 –1814 service.

1849   - Punjab annexed to British India.
       - Charles Henry Harrod opens small grocery
           shop.

1850   - Population of London is 2.6 million
       - Chelsea Embankment under construction
       - Isaac Singer invents automatic sewing
           machine

1851   - Joseph Paxman designs Crystal Palace for
           the Great Exhibition
       - Second Full National Census in England and
           Wales
       - Gold discovered in Victoria, Australia.

1854   - Charge of the Light Brigade at Balaklava.
       - Crimean Battles of Alma, and Inkerman.
       - First divorce laws passed
       - Civil Registration starts in Scotland
       - St Mary's Graveyard closed in Watford.
           Fearnley Street cemetery newly
           opened.
       - First Cambridge V Oxford University boat
           race on the Thames.

1855   - Battle of Sevastopol in the Crimea.
       - Victoria Falls discovered in northern
           Rhodesia by Dr Livingstone.

1856   - Steel converter invented by Henry Bessemer.

- Ann Norris, wife of Thomas Norris dies of old
  age in Watford.
- Thomas becomes a Chelsea In-Pensioner.
- Victoria Cross first instituted.

1857 - Indian Mutiny breaks out in Bengal.

1858 - Bell of Big Ben is cast in May weighing 16
  tonnes
- Thomas Norris dies of bronchitis at Royal
  Chelsea Hospital and is buried at
  Brompton cemetery.

Epilogue

Epilogue

It is now almost two centuries since these terrifying and courageous scenes were played out beneath the burning Spanish sun: the brave actions of soldiers of so many European nations, each fighting for a cause they believed in. The French saw themselves as liberators, bringing democracy and republic to the oppressed masses of the countries they invaded – the Spanish and Portuguese were unwilling to accept an imposed monarchy and a different way of life. Britain understandably feared for her own shores. It is often this pride of nations and the desire to preserve our heritage that spurs most to action at the hardest of times. Our national pride is made obvious in Europe, with so many countries crammed on to a relatively small patch-worked continent, struggling for space, recognition and at times, supremacy. We each like our differences to be noticed easily, with flags, anthems, languages and customs. These can appear strange and unnecessary to others and yet they are so close to our own inner hearts. How many people do you know without a military background who stand to attention and salute the Union Jack when the national anthem is played? And what effects have the sound of well-played bagpipes, a rousing bugle or the steady beat of a drum? We simply cannot help it; it is in our blood. Many terrible battles have scarred the face of Europe in the years since Napoleon's demise, but only after a lasting peace of some 40 years on the continent did a war eventually break out in the Crimea. This time Britain and France stood shoulder to shoulder united as allies against a common enemy in Russia. For all the hatred and blood lust of the Peninsula, the two nations eventually began to tolerate, understand and respect each other. They finally learned that their differences are often their strengths and that these differences are far more important to those who have them, than to those who look on.

A prolonged period without war allowed the development of better international relations, industrialisation, growth of economy and the development of a more civilised and stable society. Medicine, engineering and public works flourished and in time the common man was far better off for it. This was a time before photography and so the images we see are often paintings of starchy aristocrats rather than of common people. This blurs the picture most of us have of the period and one almost believes everyone looked and behaved in a very prim and proper, over-mannerly way. Such apparent behaviour was encouraged as "Britishness" in the Victorian era and we are now left with this rather unfeeling British stereo-type. Our stiff upper lips are not however held in pride of ourselves, rather in fear of letting down those who have gone so gloriously before. By holding our emotions as we so famously do, we British sometimes we lose sight of why we have them. We should remember that tears come easily at scenes of pain and sorrow, but are most difficult to contain when they are provoked by the love of our nation and the humanity of our fellow mankind. Daft ideas abound that somehow, we insult others by flying our Union Jack. We forget that it did not fly alone on those classical and modern battlefields, it was supported by the proud colours of other nations against common enemies, which, one by one we fought and overcame together. Our flag should maintain its colourful individuality, but looks all the better when closely surrounded by those of other equally proud countries. These are nations we should never have cause to fight on the beaches.

The many years of peace enjoyed in Europe in the wake of battles in the Peninsula and following the two world wars of more modern times, are the great testament and legacy left to our nations by the brave souls who still lie buried in those far off poppy-covered fields, which remain so distantly and forever, over the hills and far away.

The Middlesex Regiment flag flies high above the ramparts at Salva-tierra de los Barros (near La Albuera) for the first time on Wednesday 18th May 2005, where we had lunch with Celia before our return journey

home. The regimental colours of maroon and yellow are said to resemble the "blood in the sand" by some. Others prefer to describe them more endearingly as their beloved "Rhubarb and custard".

Acknowledgements

Acknowledgements

Genealogical Research and Information Sources:
Brian Norris (My uncle)
Watford Registry Office, Clarendon Road, Watford.
Watford Museum, Lower High Street, Watford.
The Public Library, High Street, Watford.
County Records Office, The Goldings, Hertford.
St Catherines House, Holborn, London.
The Family Records Centre, Islington, London.
The Public Records Office Kew.
The Church of Latter Day Saints, Utah, USA.
British Railways Archive, St Pancras, London.
British Waterways Archive, Hemel Hempstead, Herts.
Paul Johnson, Image Library Manager, The National Archives.
Tim Padfield, Copyright Officer, Lord Chancellor's Advisory Council.
Royal Hospital Chelsea, Chelsea, London.
Brompton Cemetery, Old Brompton Road, Kensington.
The National Army Museum.
Mr Vivash, Watford Borough Council Cemeteries Office.
Audrey Walker, Channel Islands Family History Society, Jersey, C I.
The Society of Genealogists.

Places of Worship:
St Peters Church, High Street, Berkhamsted, Herts
St Marys Church, New Road, Northchurch, Herts.
Cyril Hasting, Deputy Ward, St James Church, High Street, Bushey.
St Mary's Parish Church, Watford.
St Mary the Virgin Parish Church, Henley-On-Thames, Oxon.
Holy Trinity Church, Trinity Parish, Jersey, Channel Islands.

Military Establishment:
Colonel Peter Knox OBE.
Gerry Patmore, Enfield Branch, The Middlesex Regiment.
Major REB Morris – The Middlesex Regiment
Major D. Bradley – PWRR Forebear Regiments Secretary.
Mike Ward – Editor, 'Die Hard' Magazine.
Brigadier Richard Holmes CBE TD.
The Middlesex Regimental Museum, The Keep, Dover Castle, Kent.
The Buffs Regimental Museum, Canterbury, Kent.
Hugh. M.du Lohan, Middlesex Regiment
Greve de Lecq Barracks, Jersey, Channel Islands.
Captain Cardona and Sergeant Garcia, 2nd Tank Company, The 16th Spanish Mechanised Regiment.

Napoleonic Period Specialists & Re-enactors:
Stephen Voller, Napoleonic modelling specialist.
Jim Harlow, Napoleonic Re-enactment & Uniforms.

Rob Anderson, 88th Connought Rangers.
Ronald Brighouse, Napoleonic Association Liaison &
71st Lt Infantry
Anne Belsey, Uniforms Specialist (Coldstream Reg't of
Foot)
Nancy Dench, The Sutlers Stores, Bournemouth.
Ed Parker, The Napoleonic Association UK.
Brian Fosten, Napoleonic uniforms expert.
Tim Rose and the 'Die Hards' Victorian Re-enactment
Regiment. – Photographs.
6th Cacadores, Portuguese Napoleonic Association.

Friends in Spain and Portugal:
Celia Denney, Secretary of the Friends of Elvas.
Major Nick Hallidie, Chairman of the Friends of Elvas.
Don Manuel Diaz Gonzalez, the Major of La Albuera.
Miguel Angel Gomez Madera
David Diaz Gomez
Alfredo Soriano Ferrera
Maria Nieves Benegas Rivero
Celestino Velenciano
Domingo Dominguez Llavador
Jose Manuel Gomez Hormigo
Jose Antonio Gomez Madera
Manolo Gomez Madera
Piedad Garcia Galván
Juan Fernando Diaz Gomez
Cristian Gómez Gónzalez
Sheila Gómez Gónzalez
Abel Soriano
Jessi Tournier
Maria Carmen Paté Flores

Rocio Belmonte Llavador
Belen Belmonte
Antonio Goye
Juan Miguel Lopez Gomez
Antonia Gomez Garcia
Maria Isabel Rubio Garcia
Toui Gomez Garcia
Cristina Lopez Gomez
Maria José Gonzalez Gomez
Eva Morales Gomez
Maria Carmen Perez
Remedio Piriz Cañún
Elena González Bermejo
Enrique Gonzalez Cardoso
Regino y Maribel
Lidia Sãeue Marquez
Rufino Diaz Espinosa

Miscellaneous:
Jamie Thornton – Artwork for book cover
Trevor Hacking, initial proof reading.
Linda Hacking – travel arrangements and Spanish translations.
BBC Three Counties Radio, promotions.
Graham Cook, Writersworld Publishing.
Stuart Hacking, image scanning.
Joseph Bekerman, Thornhill, Ontario, Canada.
MGS Medal Photographs.
Matt Hemley, Watford Observer Newspaper.
Paul (John Quixote) Norris – photography and filming in Spain

Sylvia Norris and George Clark, for their encouragement.
Abbie, Sadie and Alfie, for their patience.

Bibliography

Bibliography

Infantry Uniforms 1742-1855 by R&C Wilkinson-Latham.

Osprey Men at Arms Series (Infantry 1) by Brian Fosten

The Napoleonic Wars, by Bernard Cornwell.

The Great Commanders, Channel 4 History.

The Thin Red Line, by Donald and Brian Fosten.

Years of Victory 1802-1812, by Arthur Bryant.

Kings and Queens of England, by R.Castleden.

World History – Brockhampton Press.

The New Standard Encyclopaedia, Odhams Press 1932.

The New Illustrated Universal Reference Book, Odhams Press 1933

The Middlesex Regiment, Alec Powell 2002.

The Book of Watford by J.B.Nunn.

Los Sitos de Badajoz y La Batalla de la Albuera, T.G. Robinson. 1998.

Recreacion Historica, Excmo Ayuntamiento de La Albuera y Junta de Extremadura Consejeria de Cultura, 2002.

The Story of Spain by Mark Williams 1999